COMIC B

AND PRICE GUIDE

Collecting Tips · Wealth Creation · Critical Reviews · Survival Information

Sanjiv Purba & Sandy Sicilia

Published by Hobby House Press, Inc.
Grantsville, Maryland
www.hobbyhouse.com

Acknowledgements

We want to express our gratitude to comic book creators and the comic book publishers who have created a wonderful world of fantasy and imagination for everyone to enjoy.

We are especially grateful to Dark Horse for their early support in this venture. They have been incredibly helpful. We also want to thank Dark Horse Comics, Inc., Twentieth Century Fox, Carol G. Platt, and Lucasfilm Ltd for permission to use comic book covers on the front of this publication.

We want to especially express our very special thanks to the following individuals who really went above and beyond the call of duty in assisting us:

Shawna Ervin-Gore, Lee Dawson, Amy Huey - Dark Horse Comics, Inc.

Janie Freedman - Twentieth Century Fox

Carol G. Platt - Marvel Enterprises, Inc.

Christopher Holm, "Chris Cerasi" - Lucasfilm Ltd.

Special thanks to Alexander, Christian, Naveen and Neil for occasional fact clarification.

Sanjiv Purba
Sandy Sicilia

Additional copies of this book may be purchased at $19.95 (plus postage and handling) from
Hobby House Press, Inc.
1 Corporate Drive, Grantsville, MD 21536
1-800-554-1447
www.hobbyhouse.com
or from your favorite bookstore or dealer.

Printed in the United States of America

ISBN: 0-87588-645-0

Table of Contents

Introduction

Comic books represent many things to different people. They are an art form, a reflection of society, an escape from reality, an expression of human creation, a learning tool, and an avenue for generating wealth. These are the positive perceptions that people have of the hobby. Some negative perceptions are held by people who find them to be time consuming, space consuming, a financial quagmire where only a few earn money, and a place for wacky and weird imaginations to run wild. What is the true answer? We believe it to be somewhere in the middle with a strong leaning towards the positive attributes.

Welcome to the comic book survival and price guide. Collecting comic books is a popular hobby around the world. This is an ongoing periodical that is dedicated to providing comic book collectors with vital information about their hobby from insiders, including what's hot, what's not, commentary, reviews, opinions, price ranges, and wealth-creation strategies. The content is provided by fans, enthusiasts, dealers, and comic book creators.

We separate ourselves from other comic book price guides by focusing on building near complete lists of popular characters and special events. The first issue of this guide focuses on providing survival information that is vital for comic book readers to get the most out of this hobby. Our price guide portion focuses on first appearances, first issues, special issues, and some hard-to-find comic related items. Special issues include cameos, guest appearances, specific creators, death, birth, marriage, and other special events.

The focus of this ongoing periodical is to:
- Help you maximize your enjoyment from this hobby.
- Reflect on this hobby's value to society.
- Provide you with the knowledge to make good buying and selling decisions.
- Capture comic book history.

Given these objectives, why are we including comic book pricing as well? After all, there are other well-known price guides available. It's impossible for any single guide to cover the needs of all collectors without being thousands of pages in length. We are addressing other unfulfilled needs in the marketplace with the following focus areas:
- Our pricing averages are weighted with Internet auctions and temporary price spikes are removed.
- We are tracking books that are expected to do well in terms of price appreciation because of their strong ties to the public media, such as motion pictures and television programs.

- We focus on providing extensive and comprehensive lists for collectors to use as checklists:
  - Spider-Man is the focus of this book. We have built a detailed list of Spider-Man appearances and cameos as well as villains and special events. This allows readers to search by character name, as opposed to having to look under a set of different headings (e.g. *Marvel Team-Up*, *Amazing Spider-Man*, and *Spectacular Spider-Man*).

- We are including other lists, such as first character appearances and generally collected artists as well as a reference to the work that we feel made them famous.
- We will continue including items that have historical value, which may not be priced elsewhere.
- Future volumes of this book will continue with the model of including pricing by major character - sorted by the character and not by book title. We will also continue to include lots of different types of lists.

Captain Victory #1 PC Comics Jack Kirby explains the meaning of "Victory is Sacrifice" in this founding series for Pacific Comics.

Comics, Society, and Television

The comic book hobby has never lived in isolation. It has always been a reflection of society, and has in turn influenced popular culture. This is a theme we are going to continually explore in this book. For example, the Great Wars (World War I and II) were represented in the early comic books – notably the ones created by Simon and Kirby (see *Boy Commandos #2*, 1943 or *Boys' Ranch #4*, 1951). Jack Kirby captures the horrors and heroism of World War II in many of the characters he works with, especially Captain America. Jack Kirby summed up the experiences of the World Wars in his definitive creation *Captain Victory and the Galactic*

Captain America 2
Marvel Comics
Captain America was a powerful symbol of democracy in the Second World War.

Rangers in a single line, "Victory is sacrifice."

The conflicts of the 1960s were captured in the pages of the *Amazing Spider-Man*, *The Incredible Hulk*, and the *Fantastic Four*. Here we saw class conflict, the Vietnam War, and the growth of the hippy culture and flower power. But not everything was about change. The other half of society continued to long for the basic flavors of life. Superman and Batman stories continued to reflect the straightforward values of the 1950s – a straightforward delineation of good versus evil.

Comic books have continued to evolve with society. The music, fashion, and openness of the 1970s were reflected in their pages. Especially noteworthy was the

WitchBlade 1
Image Comics
Start of the popular *WitchBlade* series.

X-Men 130
Marvel Comics
Origin of the mutant Dazzler, who
went onto get her own series.

Iron Man VI #182
Marvel Comics
Iron Man, or specifically Tony Stark,
is a longtime study on the effects of
alcoholism.

reflection of women and minorities
in important and heroic roles. Ms.
Marvel, Spider-Women, the Dazzler,
Black Canary, and Red Sonja
emerged to star in their own
monthly series. The Black Panther,
Black Lightning, and the Falcon
similarly moved from being sidekicks
or unknowns to the stars of their
own books.

As the 1980s emerged, the
comic book hobby began to reflect
the self-centered attitude of that
materialistic decade. The demand for
comic books increased as collectors
and speculators started buying them
in the hopes of making a lot of
money. We didn't ask for good
stories, but rather what was hot and
what would go up in value.

A single copy of a comic book
was no longer good enough, so we
bought multiple copies for investment purposes. This fueled a strong
growth in the comic book industry
in terms of publishers, distributors,
and dealers. We saw our own
dot.com meltdown 12 years earlier
than the rest of the world with the
rise and fall of the independent black
and white comic book market.

While Madonna's *Material Girl*
song reflected the 1980s attitude in
popular music, a single Iron Man
comic book issue that showed Tony
Stark waving a wad of credit cards as
a solution to all of his problems sum-
marized so much of the society at
large. That panel, in fact, looked so
cool at that time.

After peaking in sales in 1993, comic books struggled to remain relevant, perhaps as much as other cultural facets of the 1980s. The big comic book companies started losing money and canceling titles. We started to see the opposite of the growth trend of the 1980s. Collectors began to lose hope. Was their love for this medium misplaced? Were computers, the Internet, and the World Wide Web the new equivalent of the comic book for generation X? Was the printed page going to be forever replaced by virtual pages? After all, even Stan "The Man" Lee was dabbling in online comics.

In fact, the Internet, with its ability to bring communities together, fueled resurgence in the popularity of the comic book hobby. Collectors were suddenly buying and selling online. Online auctions like eBay™ and Amazon.com provided a forum for anyone and everyone to trade – sometimes at incredibly attractive prices.

Then came the *X-Men* and the *Spider-Man* movies. Both of these broke box office expectations and

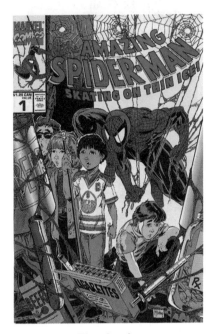

***Skating on Thin Ice* I**
Marvel Comics
A public service announcement type story starring Spider-Man.

captured a new generation of fans, as well as recapturing the imagination of former comic book hobbyists that had strayed. Many more comic-related movies are in production.

Frequently Asked Questions

Comic fans and non-fans alike have a lot of questions to ask about the hobby. You hear these in comic book stores, on the street, in bookstores, and in movie theatres. Some of the interesting ones are included here.

Q: What is a blue chip comic book?

A: This depends on the answer to a set of questions. Has the book's writer or artist been in demand for a long time? Has the title character become part of the popular culture so much that it is a licensed product? Does the title character appear in an ongoing comic book series preferably one that has been published for years? Does the comic book belong to a title that has enough of a fan base to survive bad economic or storytelling times? These are

8

some of the questions that should be asked before committing to long term investing in a comic book series or title. There is more on this topic later in this book.

Q: Who collects comic books?

A: People from every conceivable demographic collect comic books.

Q: How much should I spend on my comic book collection?

A: This depends on what you want to collect and for what purpose. To start, spend any amount that will not affect your lifestyle. Only spend what you can afford.

Q: Can we actually make money buying and selling comic books?

A: Absolutely, and you can do so whether you're a comic book dealer or a collector. However, you must follow certain basic rules otherwise you can also lose money. You must never forget the importance of the enjoyment and value factor. There are very few hobbies where you spend money, get the enjoyment, and have a product to resell at a potentially higher value.

Q: How do I become a comic book creator?

A: Figure out what your talent is and start working. For example, are you a potential penciller, inker, colorist, or are you a writer? Perhaps you are a combination of a few of these? Show your work to comic book creators and editors at conventions to get professional feedback. Write letters to the editor to become better known.

Q: What is so important about connection to the popular media?

A: The popular media, which we'll define as motion picture movies, television (both cartoons and live action shows), video games, and print have a tremendous influence on the buying patterns of the consumer. When people see a character in a big-budget movie, they are more likely to buy products based on that character either as gifts or for themselves.

Q: Who are the best-known comic book fans?

A: Jerry Seinfeld comes to mind immediately. Almost every one of the episodes of the popular *Seinfeld* series that takes place in Jerry's apartment shows a glimpse of a Superman statue or image in the background. Nicholas Cage is another well-known collector.

Q: What is comic book acidity and how do you stop it?

A: This naturally occurs in paper and causes it to change color and deteriorate over time. If you put your comic book in a plastic bag and leave it, the process will start on its own and begin to damage the book. Even the plastic bag starts to help the process by locking the paper acids into the space. The process of deacidification involves removing naturally occurring acid from the paper stock. Some ways to combat acidity include changing storage bags regularly (throw them away – don't reuse them), using acid-free backboards next to the comic book paper, using acid free storage bags (e.g. Mylar), get a professional to deacidify a comic book.

Terminator/Robocop
Dark Horse Comics
We love Dark Horse's ability to bring diverse properties into a single story!

The Spectacular Spider-Man 158
Marvel Comics
Bring on Superman or Spawn!

Blue Chip Comic Books

A "blue chip" stock is one that is based on solid economic fundamentals and business principles that will just about ensure that the stock's value will increase over time – generally higher than the rate of inflation and average interest. Just like the stock market, the comic book hobby offers a set of books that can be considered to be "blue chip". These are books that are based on characters, creators, and other characteristics that make the book series much sought after by collectors. They are also better able to weather any storms that may arise from time to time in the hobby.

For example, the cover of *Silver Surfer* VI #4 is a classic depicting a fight between two powerful heroes.

This book is originally priced at 25¢ and now lists for $750 in NM+ condition. This would have been quite a successful investment. The term "blue chip" can refer to individual comic books or to the series itself. For example, it is safe to say that *Swamp Thing* #20 (first Alan Moore work) is a blue chip comic, but the series itself is not. Meanwhile the entire *Iron Fist* series V1 #1-15 can be considered blue chip.

Other characteristics of blue chip comic books include:

- Long lasting series with significant characters (e.g. *Fantastic Four*)
- Main-stream media exposure (e.g. tie-ins to movies and television)
- Major impact on a significant character (e.g. *Secret Wars* #8 is the first appearance of Spider-Man's black suits)
- Special contribution by a comic book creator (e.g. *The Mighty Thor* V1#181 Neal Adams art, *Amazing Spider-Man* V1 #298 Todd McFarlane)
- Low distribution of a comic in a popular series (e.g. *Silver Surfer* V1#4)

Silver Surfer V1#4
Marvel Comics
Our money's on Thor! This book had limited distribution and is perpetually hot.

Using this criteria list as a basis, for example, some of books that can be considered as examples of blue chip collectibles along with the key reason why include the following:

- *Brave and Bold* V1 #28 — Origin of the Justice League of America
- *Batman* V1 #1 — 1st issue of the Batman series.
- *Fantastic Four* V1 #1 — 1st book of the Marvel Age.
- *X-MEN* V1 #94 — 1st appearance of the New X-Men in the regular title.
- *X-MEN GS* V1 #1 — 1st appearance of the New X-Men.
- *Incredible Hulk* V1 #181 — 1st full Wolverine story.
- *Daredevil* V1 #168 — 1st appearance of Electra.
- *Daredevil* V1 #1 — 1st appearance of Daredevil (subject of a big screen movie)
- *Avengers* V1 #4 — 1st modern appearance of Captain America.
- *Iron Fist* V1 #1 — 1st issue of the character and John Byrne art.

Some comic book series that can be considered as blue chip are as follows:

- *Amazing Spider-Man*
- *X-Men*
- *Avengers*
- *Fantastic Four*
  Iron Man
- *Thor*
- *Brave and the Bold*
- *Showcase*
- *Hulk*
- Any mainstream Golden Age superhero title brings a very good price today if the comic is in decent condition (e.g. Fine+ or 6.5 and up)

X-Men 94
Marvel Comics
An autographed copy of the second appearance of the *New X-Men*.

Avengers V1 4
Marvel Comics
1st Silver Age appearance
of Captain America.

Iron Fist 1
Marvel Comics
Cool cover and great
John Byrne art.

Daredevil 1
Marvel Comics
Look for this issue to
appreciate in value as
Daredevil hits the big
screen.

Chapter 1:
Ten Basic Survival Rules

What's so hard about collecting comic books? After all, you buy the comics you want, build up a collection, and then sell it for a profit some day. Right? Well not exactly. There is something different about this hobby that makes it far more complicated. Once someone begins to enjoy comic books, chances are that they will be fans permanently, despite occasional lapses in interest. At times they will go on vacation and look for comic books at foreign shopping malls with their significant others along for the ride. At some point, they may decide to go on a back-issue buying binge and buy an entire collection of the *Invincible Iron Man* Volume I in a span of a few weeks. They may end up spending hundreds of dollars (give or take) a week on the hobby.

Then all of a sudden they may decide they've outgrown comic books and start selling portions of

Action Comics #23
DC Comics
First Lex Luthor appearance.

the collection at a fraction of what was paid to acquire it. Then suddenly they will happen to see a comic book issue by chance and remember what was attractive about the hobby in the first place. The collecting interest may start up all over again, but with great regret because the copies that were sold so hastily may be worth so many times more since the sale. For example, in 1990, a copy of the *Amazing Spider-Man* V1 #1 sold for $3000 in NM condition. That same NM copy could sell for $70,000 today.

After many decades of collecting and serving comic book readers and collectors, we have been able to draw some basic survival rules that will help you navigate through the challenges posed by this hobby. Here are ten rules you should follow in this hobby to maximize your enjoyment, minimize regrets, and make some money along the way:

1. Collect comic books that you enjoy reading
2. Sell when a comic book is hot
3. Never sell when you need money – if you can avoid it
4. Never sell when you lose interest in the hobby
5. To create wealth, speculate on "blue chip" items that nobody wants today, but may want tomorrow
6. Avoid buying a comic when it is red hot because its price can decline significantly
7. Educate yourself on grading comic books
8. Learn to recognize restored comic books and other anomalies
9. Find a trustworthy dealer
10. Protect your collection

1. Collect comic books that you enjoy reading.

This is a standard rule for everything you do. By enjoying what you're doing, you're enjoying the process and you win regardless of the outcome. Your enjoyment of the hobby is the biggest bargaining chip you have when selling your collection. If you are happy with your collection, you will be more likely to hold onto it until you get the price that you desire from potential buyers. It's like owning property and not having to sell until you get your price.

Face it, comic books are too expensive to allow most collectors to buy everything that is being published every month. Before the mid-1980s, a relatively finite number of comic books were printed every month at a price less than a dollar or so each. A $20 investment could pretty much buy you everything you wanted. The current price of a comic book ranges between $2.00 and $5.00 on average. Despite the adjustments to earned salaries since that time, this is still a hefty price to pay if you were to buy most of the monthly books being published today.

Amazing Spider-Man #59
Marvel Comics
An early MJ appearance. By the way, those boots were very popular in the 1960s.

TOR #1
DC Comics
DC's answer to *Conan the Barbarian* perhaps?

The Brave and The Bold #187
DC Comics
The Metal Men are kind of like the Seven Dwarves from Snow White.

Amazing Spider-Man #1, V3
Marvel Comics
John Byrne has written new origin stories for some of the most popular comic book characters.

Marvel Two-in-One #96
Marvel Comics
This is one of the best comic book stories we've ever read. You'll love the ending.

2. Sell when a comic book is hot.

Just like stocks and real estate, comic book prices fluctuate due to a wide number of factors. One of these is demand. This is a measurement of how quickly a comic book can be sold for cash. You want to sell when there are lots of people looking to buy a particular book or series. You'll get a better price from a dealer who can also count on a quick sale to their customers.

Two months before the 1989 *Batman* movie starring Michael Keaton came out, you could not find a dealer to buy 1980s *Batman* appearance books (e.g. *Detective*, *Batman*, etc.) even at cover price – generally 40¢ or 50¢.

A month after the big budget movie was a smashing success at the box office, a collector could effortlessly sell their entire collection of the same *Batman* issues to just about any dealer at well over cover price a piece. A year after the movie came out, the books were still worth the higher value in the price guides, but a collector could not find a dealer willing to buy as many books and as quickly. The demand for *Batman*

World's Finest #169
DC Comics
It looks like Superman's
grown a beard too.

The Brave and The Bold #122
DC Comics
Batman and the Swamp Thing

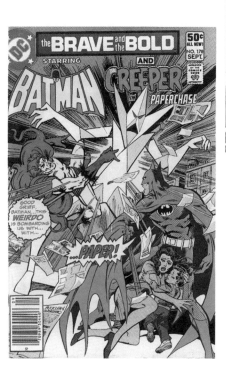

The Brave and The Bold #178
DC Comics
Batman and the Creeper

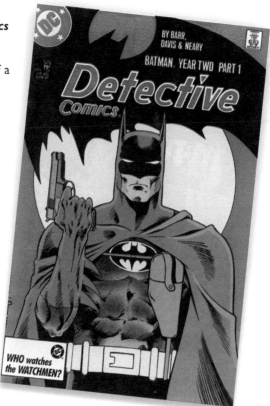

Detective Comics #575
DC Comics
The first story of a mini-series inside Detective.

merchandise had dropped significantly. Comic books sell for high value when they are liquid. They are liquid when there is high demand. This is heavily based on getting your timing right.

3. Never sell when you need money.

Comic books do not, in general, have the same liquidity as other investments like gold and stocks. These prices are well established, and while you may pick the wrong time to sell, the terms of the sale are pretty straightforward. An ounce of gold costs a certain amount regardless of how badly you need to sell it. You will find that the amounts you are offered for your comic books is inversely proportional to how badly you want to sell, or how badly the buyer wants to buy from you. Sell when you don't really want to sell and you will be surprised at the profits that can be made.

4. Never sell when you lose interest in the hobby.

A common mistake many comic book hobbyists make is to assume that they've lost interest in the hobby – or worse yet – assume they've outgrown it. The phenomenon of "outgrowing" comics is uniquely North American. Many countries, such as Japan, view comics as a vital art form and are a strong part of their cultural heritage. It is uncommon for comic book collectors to permanently lose interest in this hobby. There are certainly peaks and valleys of interest. The valleys can even last for years. However, the day inevitably comes when you pick up a comic book and suddenly remember why you loved them in the first place. Selling your collection in a valley will cloud your judgement and make you accept a low offer. From personal experience, it feels awful to reawaken the love of comics after selling your collection for 10% of its value.

5. To create wealth, speculate on "blue chip" items that nobody wants today, but may want tomorrow.

This doesn't mean that you should collect crap. But then again, who really determines what falls into that category. When the dot.com stock market was driven by what Federal Reserve Chairman Alan Greenspan called "irrational exuberance," stocks with good Price to Earnings ratios and solid futures – like banks, energy, and retail stocks – were being sold at huge discounts by investors who wanted to pay big dollars for hot stocks that had no immediate futures. The same holds true for comic books.

When the public is scrambling for that *Teenage Mutant Ninja Turtle* issue or *Fish Police* #1 (both really good books, but the prices fluctuate wildly), consider picking up issues of solid stocks like *Silver Age Avengers*, *Thor*, *Fantastic Four*, *Flash*, *Green Lantern* or *Iron Man*. This is also called counter-culture investing.

Also consider buying key issues such as 1st appearance of ongoing characters like *The Black Cat*, *Gambit*, and *Rogue*. The prices are still affordable with a strong upside potential.

6. Avoid buying a comic when it is red hot because its price can decline significantly.

What do the *Death of Captain Marvel* #1 graphic novel and Peter Parker the *Spectacular Spider-Man* #28 and #29 all have in common? Although the books have several things in common, what is pertinent to this discussion is that they all enjoyed a triple digit increase in price between one price guide and its next edition ($25, $28, $28 respectively). All three books subsequently lost a large portion of their value over the years and have never gone back to the same price. Here are a few more examples: *GI Joe* V1#1 (peak price $25), *Marvel Fanfare* V1#1 (peak price $15), and *Fish Police* V1#1 (peak price $150). If you're going to buy a hot book at a high price, do it for the right reason, such as filling out a collection. Be prepared to hold onto it. It is likely to go down and may take a long time to climb back up again.

7. Educate yourself on grading books.

Grading is a common process across many collectibles based hobbies. It involves physically inspecting a collectable piece and assigning it a grade based on its condition. Coins, stamps, and cards can all be graded. Comic books are unique among collectibles in that they are intended to be read and hence handled by the

Venom 1
Marvel Comics
From the pages of Spider-Man, it's the costume on a criminal.

FF VI #31
Marvel Comics
Reading copy of an old *Fantastic Four* comic book. It would be worth a lot more in better condition.

buyer. They are relatively large, and extremely fragile. Excessive handling will dramatically decrease the price of a comic book.

Grading a comic book describes the process of determining its physical condition in terms of such things as cover gloss, rips, tears, and creases. Since this is not a scientific process, but interpretation based on a set of rules, a comic may in fact get different grades from different people. The price difference between the same comic book in a set of different grades is staggering. Top graded books get many times the value of a book in average condition. The price of a comic book is inherently related to its condition.

8. Learn to recognize restored comic books and other anomalies.

Comic books can be repaired or restored by experts to enhance their condition. Books that are restored are worth much less than equivalent books that were not restored. The restoration process is usually not inexpensive, but some of the more expensive books (e.g. *X-Men* VI#1) can justify the cost of restoration.

Books can be restored through a variety of techniques including the addition of new paper materials. Since the price of a comic book is inherently related to its condition, it is possible to buy two low grade comic books with different sets of defects and combine the best pages from both books into a single excellent copy. For example, one book is a coverless *X-Men* V1#1, while the other book is an *X-Men* V1#1 that has a good cover but a damaged interior. However, the rebuilt book is still considered restored and worth less than an unrestored copy. Depending on the extent of the restoration, a full grade drop is a good place to start for doctored books. Learn to look for these and other types of anomalies that detract from the value of a comic book.

An anomaly in the comic book universe is only bad if it detracts from the value of the book. In fact, there are some anomalies that should actually be sought out because they add to the demand of the book. Common among these are printing errors and multiple original covers. In the Marvel Spotlight examples, can you spot the difference between the two comic books (answer: one has a #1 the other has a printing error where the issue number was not printed).

9. Find a trustworthy dealer.

The best contact you can have in the collecting hobby is to find a dealer who is trustworthy, fair, and who makes a profit from you while giving you a fair price and great service. Without the profit, the

Marvel Spotlight V2 1 with stamp
Marvel Comics
Copy of *Marvel Spotlight* V2 #1 with no printing defects.

Marvel Spotlight V2 1 without stamp
Marvel Comics
Can you spot the print defect? The "1" is missing.

The Mighty Thor #168
Marvel Comics
Water is a big enemy of comic books.

X-Men #3 in a bag
Marvel Comics
Well-protected comic book from a classic series.

dealer won't be around to sell you top quality comic books. Collectors tend to become volume oriented, which means that they can easily buy several hundred books a month during their high activity periods. It is almost impossible to check each of the interior pages individually for every book you want to buy. You must be able to trust the dealer to sell you a sound product, or replace it should you find it to be defective after the purchase.

The dealer must also be fair in giving you the best quality and type of books, and not just let you see the average merchandise. Another sign of trustworthiness is that the dealer uses the same guidelines for grading whether he buys or sells books.

10. Protect your collection.

Comic books are made from paper. They wrinkle and tear easily. Water and temperature are enemies, as are a hundred other physical threats. Left alone, the paper begins to turn yellow, then brown with age. Take the precautions to protect your collection. Remove all tape from plastic bags before removing or inserting comic books. Also, don't fold the comics when you read them. Turn the pages carefully and be sure your hands are clean before handling the pages. Don't put your coffee mug on top of a comic book pile. In addition, store them in bags with backboards to protect the spine and so that they do not bend over. Finally, store them in boxes in a cool dry place.

Chapter 2:

Comic Book Related Events

Despite the difficult economic conditions of the past couple of years, comic related items have been very hot and in high demand. The early 1990s and the mid-1980s saw similar trends where bad economic conditions had less impact on the comic book hobby than it did on other entertainment forms. Since the early 1990s, high grade Golden and Silver Age comic books have appreciated in value 10-fold. No other hobby, whether it is sports cards, coins, or stamps, can make this claim.

In the past couple of years, some extraordinary events have occurred that speak well for the future of the comic book hobby. The infrastructure has been laid to attract the next generation of collectors into the hobby through the success of the 2002 *Spider-Man* motion picture. This movie will cause a growth in new comic sales, but also a resurgence of interest in back issues.

Just how popular was the *Spider-Man* movie? It had the highest opening weekend in movie history – even adjusted for inflation – taking in $114,844,116 at the North American box office in its opening May 3, 2002 weekend. It has grossed over $403 million in the domestic box office and over $800 million worldwide – and its not finished its run yet. On an inflation-adjusted basis it has done better than *Butch Cassidy & the Sundance Kid*, *Independence Day*, *Beverly Hills Cop*, *Home Alone*, *Batman*, and the *Greatest Show on Earth*.

So how many tickets have been sold to *Spider-Man* in North America? Assuming an average ticket price of $7.00, this would mean 57,571,429 (57.5+ million) tickets in North America alone. On a global basis, *Spider-Man* has sold over 100 million tickets.

Beyond the numbers, the *Spider-Man* movie has laid the foundation for the next generation of superhero. The "kiss" is likely to go down in history as one of the most sensual in motion picture history. Look for it to be recognized in future awards ceremonies. Peter Parker and Mary Jane Watson as modern characters have appealed to a new generation of teenagers. What's particularly interesting about the popularity of this movie is that it cuts across every demographic. Adults and kids both loved it. Men and women both loved it. The movie also performed well in global markets.

Other major comic book related motion pictures also did well at the box office, including: *Star Wars: Attack of the Clones* (released May 16, 2002) which had the third largest opening weekend ever with $80,027,814; *Men in Black 2* opened with $52,148,751 on July 3, 2002.

Other comic related movies that have done well include:
- *Harry Potter*
- *Harry Potter and the Chamber of Secrets*
- *Star Wars: Phantom Menace*
- *X-Men 1*
- *Lord of the Rings: Fellowship of the Ring*
- *Lord of the Rings II: The Two Towers*

Top 10 Comic Book Related Events of the Last Decade
Here are the top 10 comic book related events of the last couple of years in no particular order (except #1).
1. The *Spider-Man* movie: enough said!
2. Comic book related television series and cartoons (e.g. *Smallville, Justice League, Batman Beyond, Zeta Project*).
3. Other major film releases including *Blade 2, Star Wars 2-Attack of the Clones, Scooby Doo.*
4. *Buffy the Vampire Slayer* series move from WB to UPN—even a network couldn't kill the vampire nemesis.

Buffy cover 1
Dark Horse Comics
Melancholy Buffy
photo cover

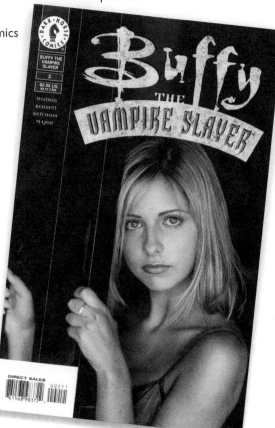

5. Marvel's return to near profitability—a healthy Marvel helps the industry.
6. J.M. Straczynski's (Joe of *Babylon 5* fame) *Spider-Man* storylines.
7. Japanese Anime Collector Cards (*Pokemon* to *Digimon* to *Yu-Gi-Oh!*).
8. Comic book related toys, bisques, and video games.
9. Sergio Aragones (*MAD* cartoonist and *Groo* creator) induction into the Hall of Fame—better than cheese-dip.
10. Revival of 1980s television series such as *Transformers* and the *Micronauts*.

Marvel *Epic Groo* 1
Marvel Comics
Groo is a satirical character from *Mad Magazine* contributor Sergio Aragones.

Transformers 1
Marvel Comics
The cover opens like a verticle window shade.

What's Next?

With more movies in the works based on comic book characters including *X-Men 2*, *Spider-Man 2*, *Daredevil*, *Superman*, *Batman*, *Star Wars*, and *The Incredible Hulk*, we can expect to continue seeing an increased interest in collecting comic books. A Batman versus Superman movie is also reportedly due out in 2004.

More television shows like *Birds of Prey* based on the Bruce Wayne fugitive story are in the works. Sony Pictures is working on an *Astro-Boy* movie. Nicolas Cage has potentially signed up to play the lead role in an upcoming *Ghost Ryder* movie.

There has been a sizeable increase in the sale of trade paperbacks that reprint older comic book material and stories. This reflects an increased interest on the part of readers to enjoy the content of comic books and not to just collect them for profit. Paradoxically, this will increase profitability by getting more buyers into the market that will likely not sell their books for a long time. Every book that enters a private collection is not on the market for years, thereby causing competition for the ones that are still in circulation.

Babylon 5 #1
DC Comics
Adaptation of the popular television science fiction series.

The Amazing Spider-Man #31
Marvel Comics
Michael J. Straczynski is a prolific writer and the mind behind *Baylon 5*. He also answers email from time to time.

We are also expecting to see an increase in the following areas over the near term:
- More video games (including online ones).
- More toys based on comic book characters as well as a continued resurgence of comic books based on toys.
- More licensing (television shows, cereals, apparel, decorations, lunch boxes).
- More focus on putting out reader friendly stories to grab new readers.

Chapter 3:

Why Comic Books are Collected

Comic book collections come in many formats and can take many forms. Some may contain tens of thousands of books, while other collections may be small enough to fit into a desk drawer. The typical collection is stored in large rectangular cardboard boxes, which are specifically designed to hold comic books, piled up in a dry, temperate corner of a collector's house.

Each box can contain 350 standard sized books depending on the volume of air that is left between the books and whether they are stored in protective bags with cardboard packing. In the latter case, about 250 books fit into the storage box.

The typical comic collection also contains odd sized books. This includes magazines, pocket sized books, and extra large books. These are often piled into other odd shaped boxes or storage containers, or occasionally piled on top of other books or stored inside drawers. Comic related items such as pewter figures, ceramic figures, busts, toys, and video games are also part of the mix.

Then there's the special stash. These are the few books that are more expensive than the rest of the collection or that have special meaning to the collector. These are often stored separately from the rest of the collection for quicker access. This could perhaps be in a metal container or storage safe that provides an additional degree of protection against hazards, natural elements, or natural disaster.

Why Comic Books are Collected

Some people like to read them, some like to collect them, and some people like to do both. Some people collect comics to relive their youth and bring back memories. People who have grown up liking comic books find that they can enjoy the hobby with their children. This is a hobby that adults and children can enjoy together – including going to the comic book store, selecting the comics, and then reading them together. This will help them grow closer together and build a bond of friendship. Other reasons include enjoyment and wealth creation.

Enjoyment

Comics are fun! They are entertaining. They bring out ideas. They are thought provoking. The combination of words, pictures, tones, and colors allows readers to escape into worlds of imagination and splendor without boundaries all

Boxed collection 1
A typical comic book collection stored in a dry, cool corner of a home

Assorted comic collection
DC & Marvel
Individually protected comic books.

the while offering something of value in all entertainment genres.

Wealth Creation

There are very few hobbies where you can learn, be entertained, and create wealth at the same time. The comic book hobby provides this opportunity. In fact, since comic books can be resold in the future, even selling them at their original cost allows you to enjoy a hobby and recoup most of the money you've spent. If you invest wisely and sell at the appropriate times, you can actually make money.

Comic book collecting for wealth generation is like a smaller version of the stock, future, and real estate markets, as it obeys the same basic rules of supply and demand with the usual twists and turns. Had many of us applied the lessons learned in comic book investing during the dot.com stock bubble, we would have recognized the right time to sell out of the market and would have made fortunes.

Here are some strategies to help you select comic books that are likely to appreciate over time:

- Invest in first appearances of characters, in addition to the first issues of the series, as the former can go up just as much or more (e.g. look at the prices of Brave and Bold #28 and Justice League #1, Amazing Fantasy #15 and Amazing Spider-Man #1 as they keep leapfrogging each other).

- Collect what other people are not interested in. When Star Wars #1 first came out, most collectors didn't know what to make of it.

- Realize that the print runs of many comic books published between 1993-2001 were extremely low as compared to print runs in the 1980s. The former could appreciate as the hobby expands.

- Pre-1970s books in high grade will become increasingly difficult to find and are a good investment.

- Buying too many multiple copies for investment can be hazardous and expensive as only ten percent or less of published comics become scarce and in great demand.

- Most comic books should give back your principle investment plus some appreciation if sold at the right time and not as a fire sale.

- Don't collect to pay for college because when that time comes it may not be the right time to sell what you've collected.

Social Commentary

Comic books are an effective reflection of society's values and the goals and dreams of entire generations. Flip through some of the older comic books and see what the past decades were like. They are almost like time machines that show snapshots of our collective history.

Many writers and artists (e.g. Frank Miller and Jim Starlin) have used comic books to speculate about different topics that affect society. Some common themes include:

- Real world culture is reflected in anecdotes.
- The effects of world wars, social unrest, women's liberation movement, prejudice, and computerization.
- Satires and allegories.
- Reflection on what is, what could have been, or what can be someday.

Art Form

Comic books use pictures and words to tell a story. Action, movement, excitement, drama, and suspense are represented in this art form and expression is the focus. Styles vary across many dimensions including country, culture, time, and comic publisher. In some countries like Japan, Italy, and Spain, comic books cut across all generations in terms of appeal. In these cultures, the comic book is a legitimate art form that is accepted by society as a whole. An adult riding a train is just as likely to be reading a comic book as a novel or newspaper. In North America, comic strips are accepted as a mainstream satire and reflection of society, but not to the extent as the other countries mentioned. With the continued box-office successes of motion pictures based on comic book characters, the trend must be in favor of comic book popularity.

Education

Comics, like other entertainment vehicles, provide an opportunity for learning. Beneath the beautiful artwork and strong story telling are a lot of different facts and lessons about life. Topics such as science, technology, sociology, history, mathematics and geography are frequently represented in comic books. Comic book heroes are often very driven and hard working people. Techniques for achievement, acceptance, understanding oneself, and understanding others are also common themes.

Chapter 4:

A Brief History of Comic Books

One of the driving objectives of this publication is to honor and reflect on comic book history. We start with an examination of genres that are reflected in comics.

Comic Book Genres and Important Dates

Many of the earliest comic book stories focused on monsters, horror, westerns and suspense. These tales were largely self-contained in that the story began and ended in the same comic book.

The introduction of superheroes started an interest in story line continuity. Even though stories could start and end in the same issue, they needed to remain consistent over time. For example, the Lone Ranger's horse's name was Silver, and it was not acceptable to have a different name for it in a future issue. Stories also became

more sophisticated and could no longer fit into a single issue. This saw the rise of the multi-issue story arc as the foundation for the modern comic book.

At the core of the modern comic book is the superhero or superheroine. They are more than a cape, costume, and a secret identity. In many ways these characters are what many people what to be at one time or another – bigger than life, adventurous, righteous, and protectors of other living beings regardless of their color or shape. These heroes value life above all else and at the same time are willing to risk themselves to save others and bring lawbreakers to justice.

Some of the major genres that have been addressed in comic book history, their first or early appearance, and the name of their publisher are shown in the following table.

Genre Title	Early, 1st, or Important Appearance	Publisher
Aviation	Wings Comics #1 sept 1940	Fiction House Mag.
Classics	Classic Comics #1 oct 1941 The 3 Musketeers	Elliot Pub
Costumed Super Heroine	All Star Comics #5 jun 1941 Hawkgirl	DC

Genre Title	Early, 1st, or Important Appearance	Publisher
Crime	Crime Does Not Pay #22 jun 1942	Comic House/Lev Gleason
Satire Comics	- Mad #1, 1952 - Mad #29 September 1956, 1st full color Alfred E. Neuman on cvr	Mad
Funnies	Famous Funnies #1 1934 First monthly newsstand comic book	Eastern Color Printing Co
Horror	Eerie #1 jan 1947 one shot	Avon
Movie Comic	Movie Comics #1 apr 1939 Gunga Din, Son of Frankenstein and others	
Occult	Super magic #1 may 1941 Blackstone the Magician	Street & Smith
Rock & Roll	Marvel Premiere #50 1979 Alice Cooper	Marvel Comics
Romance	Romantic Picture Novelettes #1 1946	Mag. Ent.
Science fiction	Planet Comics #1 jan 1940	Fiction House Magazine
Sports	Champion Comics #2 dec 1939	Harvey Publications
Superhero	Action Comics #1 june 1938 Superman	DC
Superhero Team	All Star Comics #3 winter 1940	DC
Sword & Sorcery	Conan the Barbarian #1, 1970	Marvel
Thrillers	Detective Picture Stories #1 dec 1936	Comic Mag
War	War Comics #1 may 1940	Dell
Western	Western picture stories #1 feb 1937	Comics Mag

Other important historical comic book dates are as follows:

- *New Fun Comics* #1, 1935 was the first comic to print new material
- Comics were 5¢ at one time, appropriately named: *Nickel Comics* #1, 1938
- The Phantom wore his first costume in 1938 in *Ace Comics* #11
- Donald Duck was the first solo Disney character in a comic book in 1938
- First 25¢ comic book: New York World's Fair, 1939
- 1st sports comic: *Champion Comics* #2 12/1939
- First 15¢ comic book: New York World's Fair, 1940
- 1st Super Hero Team: *All Star Comics* #3 Winter 1940
- 1st Female Superhero comic: *All Star Comics* #8 11/1941
- Walt Disney' *Comics and Stories* #27, 1942, by Western Publishing contained two stories that marked the debut of "Duck Man" by Carl Barks
- Robin was the first costumed sidekick in Detective Comics #38
- All Hero Comics (started 1943) FAW
- *Famous Funnies* was the first to reach #100 in 11/1943
- 1st television comic: *Howdy Doody* #1 Jan/1950
- 1st Golden Age comic: *Action Comics* #1 6/1938
- 1st Silver Age comic: *Showcase* #4 9/1956

Comic Book Ages

Much like the motion picture industry, comic books have their own equivalent of the silent era, the classics, and the modern box office. We like to divide these comic book ages into several categories that are discussed in this section. The ages are not written in stone, and different sources will identify different start and end dates, as well as the names given to the ages themselves.

Pre-Pre-Golden Age (1897-1938)

The Pre-Golden Age is generally considered to be the period between the early 1930s to the start of the Golden Age. This period saw the introduction of "funny" books that generally contained reprints of comic book strips. The period before this is sometimes called the Platinum Age. This has been getting an increasing amount of attention lately. Some of the key books in this time period include the following:

- *The Blackberries* (1901, 4th comic book)
- *Buster Brown and his Resolutions* (1903)
- *Buster Brown* (1906)
- *Comic Monthly* (1st monthly newsstand comic)
- *Famous Funnies*-Series 1, 1934

The Golden Age (Dates 1938 – 1955)

The Golden Age (GA) of comic books is typically defined as the period of time between the years 1938-1955. Despite earlier attempts at producing comic books in North America, this was really the start of

Golden Age book
Fawcett
A small sized copy of *Lance O. Casey* from the Golden Age.

Detective 27
DC Comics
1st appearance of Batman.

the comic book hobby in terms of contemporary influence. Many of the characters introduced during this period are still involved in new comic book stories today.

Some of the most highly valued comics are from the GA. Several factors contributed to this. Clearly a lot of time has passed since the books were published. The paper drives of the Second World War resulted in the destruction of a lot of paper products, including comic books. The quality of the paper used in the books of that era was highly acidic and relatively poor, causing many Golden Age comics to degrade rapidly over time. Any books left in high grades are consequently more difficult to find, thus causing the prices of known high-grade copies to rise dramatically.

When talking about high-grade books in the Golden Age we are often talking about surviving copies to number in the single digits, occasionally in the dozens. A comic book from the Golden Age in high grade (Near Mint to Mint) demands many multiples of the price included in this and other price guides.

The top books in terms of value (and influence as it turns out) from the GA include the following:
- *Action Comics* #1, DC
- *Marvel Comics* #1, Timely
- *Detective Comics* #27, DC
- *Superman* #1, DC
- *Batman* #1, DC

Other notable comic books from the GA include the following:
- *Flash Comics* #1, DC
- *Captain America Comics* #1, Marvel

Sensation Comics 1
DC Comics
1st appearance of Wonder Woman.

Golden Age book
Street & Smith's
A collection of fantasy stories from
August 1940.

- *Captain Marvel Adventures #1* Marvel
- *Human Torch #2*, Marvel
- *Marvel Mystery Comics #2*, Marvel
- *Wonder Woman #1*, DC
- *Famous Funnies #1*,
- *Wonder Comics #1*,
- *Sub-Mariner Comics #1*, Marvel

The Silver Age
(Dates: 1955-1969)

While the GA is important as the foundation for the comic book hobby, the Silver Age (SA) caused it to evolve into a form that is still relevant today and which attracts readers from all age demographics. There were many important books in the SA that introduced characters that are now the subject of big motion pictures and other television programs. Generally, there are more high-grade books available from the SA than the GA; however, some high-grade copies for the important books can still be measured in the dozens or hundreds in terms of copies available for sale to the public.

Some of the important books from the SA era include the following:

- *Amazing Fantasy #15*, Marvel
- *Showcase #4*, DC
- *Amazing Spider-Man #1*, Marvel
- *Fantastic Four #1*, Marvel
- *X-Men #1*, Marvel
- *Incredible Hulk #1*, Marvel
- *Brave and the Bold #28*, DC
- *Flash #105*, DC

Avengers 1
Marvel Comics
1st appearance of the
Avengers.

Strange Tales #125
Marvel Comics
Fire, water, and the thing.

Captain America 100
Marvel Comics
Re-appearance of Captain
America in the Marvel Age.

The Flash #109
DC Comics
A nice copy of a 10¢ cover comic book.

X-Men 2
Marvel Comics
An undervalued book.

- *Challengers of the Unknown #1,* DC
- *Daredevil #1,* Marvel
- *Iron Man #1,* Marvel
- *Silver Surfer #1,* Marvel
- *Showcase #9,* DC
- *Avengers #1,* Marvel
- *Strange Tales #101,* Marvel
- *Avengers #4,* Marvel
- *Strange Tales #135,* Marvel
- *Tales of Suspense #39,* Marvel
- *Strange Tales #135,* Marvel
- *Strange Adventures #205,* Marvel
- *Tales to Astonish #35,* Marvel
- *Fantastic Four #48,* Marvel
- *Journey into Mystery #83,* Marvel

The Bronze Age
(Dates: 1969-1980)

When you're talking about the Bronze Age (BA), you're essentially talking about the 1970s. There are a lot of potentially undervalued books in the BA. During the 1980s and 1990s, this era was largely neglected as collectors with investment capital bought up high-grade GA books and other serious collectors focused on buying up comic books from the 1960s. This has been slowly changing since the late 1990s especially since over 30 years have passed since the beginning of the BA.

The BA of comics has a large number of books that offer signifi-cant value in terms of potential appreciation. Some of the important

1st Appearance Warlord
DC Comics
Pre-dates *Warlord* #1.

Kamandi #1
DC Comics
Superb Kirby storytelling.

*The Amazing Spider-Man
VI #21*
Marvel Comics
Spider-Man and the Human
Torch are a popular teamup.

issues of this era include the following:

- *Detective Comics* #400, DC
- *Forever People* #1, DC
- *Conan the Barbarian* #1, Marvel
- *New Gods* #1, DC
- *Mister Miracle* #1, DC
- *Nova* #1, Marvel
- *Kamandi: The Last Boy on Earth* #1, DC
- *Marvel Spotlight* #5, Marvel
- *Marvel Feature* #1, Marvel
- *Savage Tales* #1, Marvel
- *Tomb of Dracula* #1, Marvel
- *Amazing Spider-Man* #129 (1st Punisher), Marvel
- *Incredible Hulk* #181 (1st Wolverine), Marvel
- *GS X-Men* #1, Marvel
- *Uncanny X-Men* #94, Marvel
- *Black Lightening* #1, DC
- *Cerebus* #1, Aardvark-Vanaheim
- *Star Wars* #1 (35¢ cover version), Marvel
- *The Warlord* #1, DC

The Modern Age
(Dates: 1980-present)

The Modern Age, title for title, has the largest quantity of titles and publishers to choose from and at affordable prices. There are lots of important books in the Modern Age and more are being published all the time. There are a few things to note about books from this period, however. The paper quality of books published in the 1980s on was significantly better than earlier periods and so degradation will be slower thereby more high-grade books are available in this time period. This will limit the financial growth potential of these books as a multiple of prices

listed in price guides such as this one. The print runs of comic books in the 1980s was fairly large, but not so with the books in the 1990s. There is a real potential for the 1990s books to appreciate in value because of a general shortage of these books if the number of collectors continues to grow – a very strong likelihood given the popularity of motion pictures based on comic book characters.

Some of the important books in the Modern Age include the following:

- *Teenage Mutant Ninja Turtles* #1
- *Spawn* #1, Image
- *Amazing Spider-Man* #298 (1st McFarlane art on Spider-Man), Marvel
- *Amazing Spider-Man* #300 (1st Venom), Marvel
- *Superman* Volume 2 #75, DC
- *Sandman* #1, DC
- *Watchmen* #1, DC
- *Aliens* V1 #1, Dark Horse
- *Daredevil* V1 #168 (1st Electra), Marvel
- *Wolverine Mini-Series* V1 #1-4, Marvel

We can further subdivide the Modern Age and examine some of the important events, trends, and books by decade.

The 1980s

The direction of the 1980s was established by the release of the second *Superman* movie starring Christopher Reeves. It was a brilliant, powerful, and imaginative movie that did very well at the box office and brought a lot of general attention to the hobby.

The 1980s saw the hobby mature. All of a sudden you could find retail stores – comic book stores – that were dedicated to selling comic books and related merchandise. It was an amazing feat that enough money was being spent on comic books to support many retail stores dedicated exclusively to the hobby in many cities across North America.

The 1980s were an excellent decade for the comic book hobby. The back issue market received a lot of attention and investment. Because of the growth in the number of stores dedicated to the hobby, something amazing started to happen. This was the rise of the "Direct Sales" market.

Historically, most books, including comic books, were sold on consignment. This meant that a publisher printed the number of copies they thought would sell to the public, and got these into the hands of distributors who then worked with retailers. After a certain period of time, say 3 months, unsold books were returned to the publisher who generally had them destroyed. The risk of unsold comic books, and returned copies, was entirely in the publisher's hands. This changed in the Direct Sales market. With the lucrative back issue sales market, comic book stores or dealers were able to forecast demand by their customers and would provide an order to the book publishers a few months in advance. These orders were final sales. That meant that unsold copies would be kept and paid for by the comic book store

owner who was expecting to sell them as backstock at a higher price.

With the Direct Sales market, comic book publishers were able to invest in more experimental books that would not have seen the light of day in the 1970s. Based on the number of pre-orders received from the comic book dealers, it was possible to restrict print runs to the exact number of copies known to be sold, and also to know how much money could be spent to produce the comic book. This approach was a real boon to accurate forecasting of sales. Consignment sales still existed, in fact some books in the direct sales channel also existed in the consignment sales channel. The two

X-Men VI #10
Marvel Comics
1st appearance of Kazar which eventually became a direct distribution sales series.

copies can be distinguished by the image in the bar code on the comic book. Direct sales copies generally had a superhero image in them, while books on consignment had a barcode for tracking in the distribution channel.

This decade saw several other remarkable achievements, as follows:

- The *Uncanny X-Men* became the consistent best seller month after month.
- Miller's *Daredevil* gained a loyal following.
- Miller's *Dark Knight Returns* became a movie in comic book form and contributed to the spectacular box office success of the *Batman* motion picture starring Michael Keaton.
- John Byrne lived out a childhood dream by redefining Superman in *The Man of Steel* mini-series.
- Byrne took over the reigns of the hurting *Fantastic Four* and worked on an incredible run (starting with issue VI #232) bringing the greatest back into the comic book.
- The *Teenage Mutant Ninja Turtles* inspired a motion picture that also became a hit. Everything was "Turtle Power", "Pizza", and "Cowabunga" for a couple of years.
- The rise and fall of the independent Black&White comic book market.

The 1990s

In the early 1990s, many best selling artists left Marvel and DC and started up Image Comics. Within a

Moon Knight #15
Marvel Comics
Moon Knight led the direct distribution strategy.

short period of time, Image books became the best selling in the industry. While the success of Image comics was fantastic, Marvel Comics was purchased through a stock buyout and then went through a series of successive sales. Meanwhile, new comic book prices continued to appreciate and fewer people were buying an even fewer number of comics. To be fair, there were a few inspired highlights, such as the *Death of Superman*, which received a lot of media attention and became overnight sensations.

For the most part, though, the spiral was downwards, as print runs became progressively smaller. In the 1980s, it was not unusual for an average comic book to sell 200,000 copies a month (The *X-Men* were routinely selling 400,000+ copies a month). Books selling in the 50,000 copies a month range were routinely cancelled. By the mid-1990s, it was rare to find a book selling more than a 100,000 copies a month. This meant several things. Fewer people were collecting, collectors were buying fewer multiple copies of a title (a common practice in the 1980s), collectors were not buying

***World of Krypton* #2**
DC Comics
Relatively little known mini-series from the 1970s.

***Raphael: Teenage Mutant Ninja Turtle* #1**
Mirage Studios
Cool Eastman black and white art.

***X-Men* 100**
Marvel Comics
#100 issues are usually popular milestones.

as many different titles, and many collectors went from being routine to occasional buyers.

The collective result of all of these events was an implosion in the comic book industry. A lot of the *Spider-Man* and *X-Men* comics were cancelled as a start. Many other titles across comic publishers followed this unfortunate trend. Back issue prices began to drop. Many long running series were discontinued to resurface a few months later in another volume starting at #1. Things really became confusing for a while.

Manga and Anime based characters were bright lights during this time. With the popularity of *Sailor Moon* (at one time the show's website was receiving millions of hits a month), then *Pokemon*, and *Digimon*, interest in comic book art continued to find support.

Then along came eBay™ and other Internet auction sites. In fact, the Internet as a whole had a strong impact on the industry. Comic book communities revived some of the fan interest. Online auctions captured the interest of long-term collectors who could now browse, click, and bid for long lost titles. Towards the end of the decade, rumors of live action movies based on such classics as *X-Men* being in production were

Untold Stories of Spider-Man 1
Marvel Comics
New stories of Spider-Man's early years.

Lost in Space 1
Innovation
A hit television show that became a comic, then a movie, and a comic again.

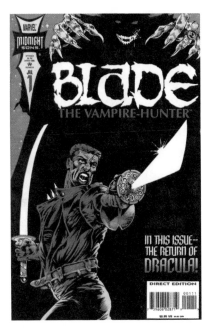

Blade 1
Marvel Comics
The comic book series that inspired the hit movies.

X-Men: Hidden Years #4
Marvel Comics
Lucky for Magneto that this is a pre-Phoenix story.

being heard. A revival of the comic book hobby was well on its way.

2000s and Beyond

The decade began with real concerns and fears about the turn of the millennium, the year 2000 computer bug, and uncertainty over the new economy. The comic book hobby was making its own revival – not in terms of sales of books, but through growing interest in comic related products. Manga and Anime based products continued to remain popular, but there was also a new buzz in the air. The *X-Men* movie starring Captain Picard himself (Patrick Stewart) and the beautiful Halle Belle was slated for a mid-summer release. The industry and collec-

tors were watching with anxiety and anticipation.

The 1989 *Batman* movie was a box office hit that helped to drive all related merchandise. However, subsequent movies, though hardly duds, did not have nearly as much impact. Could the *X-Men* movie be such a hit?

The *X-Men* movie was released to very positive reviews and performed well at the box office. The movie broke records for its 1st weekend and went on to gross a substantial amount of money. With the strength of *Blade 1* and the *Star Wars Phantom Menace* movies, comic book publishers were given some reassurance that they still owned valuable intellectual property.

Batman 10¢ (recent)
DC Comics
Not a Golden Age Comic! DC
making readers a great offer.

The Mighty Thor V3 #1
Marvel Comics
Thor Heroes Return sets the tone
for this series into the year 2000.

The Avengers V3 #1
Marvel Comics
Avengers Heroes Return sets the
tone for this series into the year
2000.

Fantastic Four V3 #1
Marvel Comics
Fantastic Four Heroes Return sets
the tone for this series into the
year 2000.

History of Cover Prices

Comic book cover prices have been experiencing escalating cover price increases over time. The following table uses *Action* and the *Amazing Spider-Man* as guides to show this trend.

Cover Date	Effective	Example	Years at Price (approximately)
10¢	Jun 1938	*Action #1*	24
12¢	Dec 1961	*Action #283*	9
15¢	Aug 1969	*Amazing Spider-Man #75*	3
20¢	Dec 1971	*Amazing Spider-Man #103*	4
25¢	May 1974	*Amazing Spider-Man #132*	3
30¢	Sept 1976	*Amazing Spider-Man #160*	2
35¢	Nov 1977	*Amazing Spider-Man #174*	3
40¢	May 1979	*Amazing Spider-Man #192*	2
50¢	Sept 1980	*Amazing Spider-Man #208*	3
60¢	Jan 1982	*Amazing Spider-Man #224*	4
65¢	Apr 1985	*Amazing Spider-Man #263*	2
75¢	Feb 1986	*Amazing Spider-Man #273*	3
$1.00	Jun 1988	*Amazing Spider-Man #301*	5
$1.25	Feb 1992	*Amazing Spider-Man #359*	3
$1.50	May 1994	*Amazing Spider-Man #389*	4
$1.95	Mar 1997	*Amazing Spider-Man #421*	.75
$1.99	Nov 1997	*Amazing Spider-Man #428*	4
$2.25	Jun 2000	*Amazing Spider-Man V2 #18*	

Chapter 5:

Editorial Comments

There are lots of things to be said about past comic books events, some positive, some negative, some simply puzzling. Let's begin this editorial section with an exploration of some of the more questionable decisions.

Questionable Decisions

To the outside world, eliminating traditional Coca-Cola and replacing it with the sweeter Pepsi-like New Coke seemed to be, well, a very questionable move. Coca-Cola had been a winning product for many decades and had outstanding brand recognition around the world. Over a decade after the event, the inside scoop shows that there was indeed some justification behind the decision that was made. We may disagree with the decision, as many people did, because the Coca-Cola Corporation reversed itself and brought the original flavor back under the title Coke Classic, but we must respect the original motivation. There have similarly been many decisions in the comic book industry that have often made us wonder "why" as well. We are sure there is an explanation as well, but still have to wonder and ask.

- Character substitution — Why was the Human Torch replaced by H.E.R.B.I.E. the robot in the *Fantastic Four* cartoon? (probably a legal reason)

- *Spider-Man* clone wars — Why turn a flagship character into a clone?
- Art style changes — We are still fans of Keith Giffen's art style in the *Legion of Superheroes* #287-302 and the *Omega Men*. Why did he change it? Why can't he go back to that style again?
- Price changes — The *New Teen Titans* was a huge commercial and literary success. Why split a successful property into a newsstand version and a direct sales version, charge more for one, and complicate the whole reprint versus original printing discussion?
- How many *X-Men* titles can a person follow? The *X-Men* storylines were some of the best of all time, but having to follow multiple timelines and continuities is too complicated.
- Multiple covers — We love comic book covers. When multiple covers came out, they were a great novelty item. Are they still selling more copies of the books?
- Platinum/Gold editions — These are great if you can get them at a low price. But what should the collectors outside the limited distribution areas do to get into the action (short of paying 100 times cover price)?

Multiple *X-Men* covers
Marvel Comics
X-Men V2 #1 variant cover.

Marvel Comics
X-Men V2 #1 variant cover.

Marvel Comics
X-Men V2 #1 variant cover.

Powerful Storylines

It's impossible to select a single storyline that could be classified as the best of all time. There are too many good ones. However, we can try to identify some powerful, outstanding, and famous storylines. These have a few things in common. They tend to span several issues. They have the same creative team. They are a reflection of society at the time of publication. They contain major changes to established characters or scenarios. Here are some examples.

- *Crisis on Infinite Earths* #1-12 — Redefined the entire DC universe combining the Golden Age, Silver Age, and multiple Earth's into a single consistent universe. Fantastic storytelling, fantastic art, and a masterpiece by Wolfman and Perez.
- *Marvel Super-Heroes Secret Wars* #1-12 — Examines the Marvel Universe through an all powerful being's perspective. Sure, the series had some minor flaws, but it introduced Spider-Man's black suit and changed a lot of characters in the Marvel Universe.
- *Wolverine* #1-4 Limited Series 1 — Contains the best of Frank Miller's style on Daredevil and applies it to one of the most popular Marvel characters.
- *Watchmen* #1-12 — In a time when accounting scandals are so prevalent, and trillions of share holder value has been lost, it is important to notice that Alan Moore & Dave Gibbons asked the famous question, "Who watches the watchers?" back in the 1980s.
- *Groo* — Contains some of the funniest and most intellectual material in comic books throughout all the incarnations of this "classic" hero.
- *The Mighty Thor* #281-300 — Who can provide a challenge to one of the most powerful Norse Gods? Well, the Celestials can. These issues essentially tie up many of the loose ends in the Thor series since *Journey into Mystery* #83 was published. This includes the reasons for Odin's treatment of Thor, the identity of Thor's mother, Thor's relationships and the future of Asgard.

Crisis 1
DC Comics
Story that began a radical rewriting of the DC Universe.

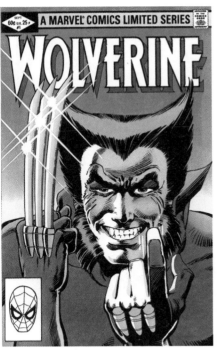

Wolverine Mini-Series V1 1
Marvel Comics
This comic reportedly sold
over 600,000 copies. Oh, and
the cover is chilling.

Thor 300
Marvel Comics
Fantastic story that explains
Thor's past, origin, and relationship
troubles.

Punisher 1
Marvel Comics
The Punisher gets his own title.
This mini series is followed by a
regular series.

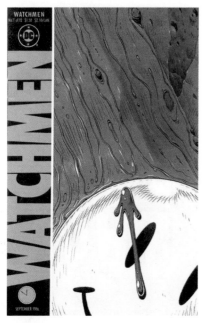

Watchmen 1
DC Comics
Possibly one of the most respected comic book stories of all time.

- *The Punisher #1-5 1st Mini Series* — Ever wonder how wonderful it would be if a superhero just blew away the really violent villains? *The Punisher* is that character. This mini-series examines Frank Castle's (aka the Punisher) past and pits him against some very nasty criminals.

Other Major Events in the History of Comics

Comic book history is covered with many significant events that had a profound impact on the hobby or some other entertainment medium. Here is a reflection on some of these events.

Adventure Comics 255
DC Comics
The Comic Code Authority logo proudly displayed in the top right corner.

I. Creation of the Comic Code Authority

In 1954, the Comic Code Authority (CCA) was created in response to increasing public and political pressure to tone down on the violent, lewd and sexual content that some comic books allegedly carried. The committee was formed by several major comic publishers to establish content guidelines. A comic book that met the guidelines was allowed to display the CCA logo on the cover. Of course, by the 1970s a comic book that did not qualify for a CCA logo actually started receiving more attention due to the obviously graphical contents.

Coyote #1
Marvel Comics
No Comic Code Authority
logo. Lots of violence.

Void Indigo #1
Marvel Comics
No Comic Code Authority
logo. Lots of violence.

Vampirella Strikes #3
Harris Comics
Always popular vampire
character. Kind of whimsical
until you notice what she's
standing on.

Bloodshot #1

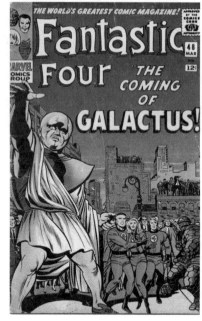

FF 48
Marvel Comics
1st appearance of Galactus and the
Silver Surfer.

2. Acclaim Entertainment buys Valiant

Acclaim Entertainment made a bold gesture to acquire Valiant for $65 million in cash and common stock in 1994. Prior to the huge market capitalization of the dot.com era, this was a spectacular amount of money to pay for a young startup company.

3. Stan Lee/Jack Kirby launch *Fantastic Four #1*

Published in 1961 with the bold and challenging title "The World's Greatest Comic Magazine," Stan Lee and Jack Kirby unleashed a new genre on the unsuspecting world. The story was about four people, not average, but still people, who wanted to do extraordinary things. They managed to get into space on their own drive and intellect, but then cosmic rays transformed them into the Fantastic Four. Having established this premise, Stan Lee and Jack Kirby then focused on the "real" problems these superhuman beings would then encounter. With this approach they changed the industry and delighted fans for over 100 beautiful issues.

4. Stan Lee/Steve Ditko launch *Amazing Fantasy* #15 starring Spider-Man

Spider-Man has been an amazing success story since the release of *Amazing Fantasy* #15 in 1962. Just about everyone should know the

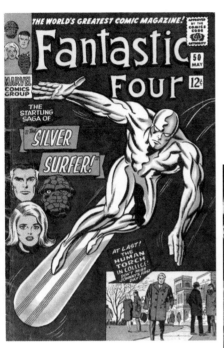

FF 50
Marvel Comics
The Silver Surfer saves
the Earth from Galactus'
ravenous appetite.

Amazing Fantasy 15
Marvel Comics
1st Appearance of Spider-Man.
Originally considered to be a
throwaway comic book.

**Spider-Man and his Amazing
Friends**
Marvel Comics
There have been many incarnations
of Spider-Man cartoons and even a
live action series.

story of Peter Parker, the shy teen, becoming Spider-Man because of the bite of a radioactive spider. *Spider-Man* the motion picture (2002) replaced radioactivity with genetic engineering. The result is still the same. Peter Parker becomes Spider-Man, becomes nasty for a brief moment that changes his life forever, and he learns that with "great power comes great responsibility."

It is important to specify the year of the *Spider-Man* movie because there have been other real-action Spider-Man movies in the past. Spider-Man has been a phenomenon for Marvel since *Amazing Fantasy* #15 (there is one caveat — see Misconceptions in Comic Book Lore that follows this section). Spider-Man's impact on cartoons, toys, and video games is staggering. As the old saying goes, "this character is just getting started after 40 years of being in the limelight!"

5. Spider-Man drug and violence issues

Over the decades, Spider-Man stories have reflected on the problems of the real world. Issues Volume I #96-98 bravely focused on drugs and the related violence. They were published without the Comic Code Authority (CCA) stamp due to the controversial content. Ignoring the topic of drugs in comic books hardly made the problem go away in the real world. Examining the topic in a written format allowed reflection and an understanding of the problems associated and caused by drug use.

6. The death of Gwen Stacy in the *Amazing Spider-Man*

In early comic books, the good guys usually won, very little changed in the way of character development, and the bad guys lost. The death of Gwen Stacy in the *Amazing Spider-Man* VI #121, Peter Parker's girlfriend and the love of his life, was a traumatic experience to many loyal fans. Many readers who are stoic about most things in their lives actually cried. Yes, we've heard this admitted on more than one occasion. From a storytelling perspective, this event cemented the realism in comic books after establishing the rules of a fictional Universe. True healing for fans may only have started after the marriage of Peter Parker and Mary Jane Watson.

7. The *Star Wars* series from Marvel and Dark Horse

It looked like a throw-away title when it first came out and so many comic book collectors ignored it. It appeared to be a Science Fiction title in a hobby dominated by superheroes, swords and sorcery, and the like. We were wrong. The first *Star Wars* series established a framework for telling compelling stories on paper, while a parallel time line was being presented at the movie box office. The comic book series expanded on the Star Wars universe, filled in some gaps, introduced solid new characters that took on lives of their own, and fed the hunger of many *Star Wars* fans that wanted more and more.

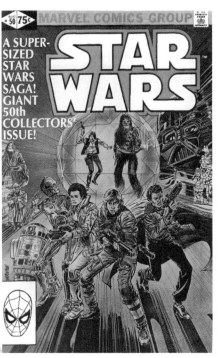

Star Wars 50
Marvel Comics
#50s are collected milestone
issues.

Star Wars 2
Marvel Comics
Star Wars V1 #2 is an under
ordered book from the
original series.

Star Wars 5
Marvel Comics
An adaptation of the 1977
Star Wars motion picture.

Star Wars 6
Marvel Comics
Star Wars V1 #6 completes
the adaptation of the 1977
hit movie.

Dark Horse *Star Wars* **1**
Dark Horse Comics
Collectors started buying
books with this character
when it became clear he was
going to be in the movies.

*Captain Marvel Graphic
Novel*
Marvel Comics
The 1st Marvel graphic novel.

8. Release of *Marvel Fanfare* and 1st Graphic Novel

There have been a lot of cover price increases in the history of comic books, but they could mostly be measured in pennies. Then along came *Marvel Fanfare* #1. In one fell swoop, an incredible slick package with 2 outstanding stories, no ads, incredible artwork, and great paper stock got a lot of collectors to fork over $1 or more without blinking. The further success of the *Death of Captain Marvel* graphic novel by Jim Starlin priced at $5.95 changed the pricing landscape forever.

As some of Chris Claremont's *X-Men* character's are used to saying, "for better or worse," the pricing acceptance by the fans allowed comic book publishers to produce really cool books with high quality paper and great covers that could be sold for higher prices. At the same time, the doors opened up for higher price increases through-out the industry.

9. *GS X-Men* #1 and the *X-Men* #94

Something strange happened with the release of *Giant Size X-Men* #1. A moribund book that had gone into reprints for dozens of issues suddenly became red hot. Even as early as 1980, some comic book retailers were SELLING *GS X-Men* for $50. In the currency of the time, this was a lot of money. *X-Men* #94 followed and there was no turning back. The *Uncanny X-Men* moved from reprint status to a consistent best seller from then on with dozens and dozens of spin offs.

10. Miller's *Daredevil*

What the *X-Men* did to the super-team, Frank Miller did to storytelling. With *Daredevil* Volume 1 #158, Frank Miller introduced a style of panel layouts, penciling, coloring and limiting the use of word balloons to tell a powerful story. The series moved from being a so-so seller into a best seller within 6 months of the release of issue #158. Of course this meant that a lot more fans were looking to buy the first couple of Miller issues for their collections, thereby pushing the price up substantially.

Marvel Team-Up #53
Marvel Comics
1st Byrne work on X-Men.

Daredevil VI #168
Marvel Comics
1st appearance of Elecktra.
Watch for her in the movies.

Daredevil 183
Marvel Comics
Drug and violence issue.

Daredevil 184
Marvel Comics
Drug and violence issue.

11. *Fantastic Four* V1 #48-50

Stan Lee and Jack Kirby were basically looking for a villain that could give the Fantastic Four a challenge for an issue or so. They ended up creating the single most intriguing super-villain of all time along with his helpers. Both of these descriptions, though, are misnomers. Galactus is a force of nature that needs to survive.

His "help" was the Silver Surfer. The Surfer was a noble and powerful creature that was drawn by Jack Kirby on a whim to act as a herald to pre-announce the arrival of the all-powerful Galactus. It was the Silver Surfer (reflective of the surfing movies and the surfer culture at the time) that caught the imagination of the reading public.

The three issues take the reader through various intellectual and emotional challenges. Earth is saved only by the noble sacrifice of the Silver Surfer who essentially adopts a sort of vegetarianism and rebels against the powerful Galactus.

Misconceptions in Comic Book Lore

There are some common misconceptions in comic book lore that are propagated throughout the industry. Someone makes a comment at a convention or a quote is published and it seems that a new fact has been established. Well, to set the record straight:

Perception 1

Myth: 1st mini-series was Marvel's *Content of Champions*
Fact: *The World of Krypton*, published by DC Comics in 1979, preceded it by several years.

Perception 2

Myth: After the success of *Fantastic Four #1*, Marvel was ecstatic about Stan Lee's *Spider-Man* concept and couldn't wait to publish it.
Fact: There is a reason why the *Amazing Spider-Man #1* is not the first appearance of this character. According to television interviews, Stan Lee was watching an ant and thought that its ability to climb walls was fascinating. But who would want a character based on ants? (quite a few if you consider the eventual success of Antman in the Avengers). He changed the character to Spider-Man, but found the Senior Editors at Marvel thought the character was too creepy for a superhero. Stan Lee put the story into *Amazing Fantasy #15* as a throwaway because it was scheduled to be cancelled. Spider-Man became a hit and got its own title.

Perception 3

Myth: Dr. Droom is a spelling mistake.
Fact: Dr. Droom is not a spelling mistake by someone trying to spell Dr. Doom, the Fantastic Four nemesis. Dr. Droom was the 1st Marvel-age superhero that appeared in *Amazing Adventures* from June 1961-Nov 1961 for 6 issues and drawn by Jack Kirby.

Chapter 6:
Comic Book Publishers

Many different publishers have produced comic books over the decades. Some are still vibrant and going strong. Others made solid contributions to the industry, but were not able to stay in business. This section provides an overview of many comic book publishers, both past and present:

Marvel

Marvel has had a tremendous impact on the comic book industry as it is known today. It started out as Timely comics. *Marvel Comics #1* is believed to be the first Marvel comic book that was published. Many books around 1960 were titled *Tales of Suspense*, *Tales to Astonish*, *Journey into Mystery*, and *Amazing Fantasy* all of which contained stories suitable for the titles. Stan Lee, Jack Kirby, and Steve Ditko changed all that by using these titles as springboards for a new breed of superhero.

Marvel followed up Spider-Man in *Amazing Fantasy* with the *Incredible Hulk*, *Strange Tales with Dr. Strange*, *The Avengers*, *Sgt. Fury*, *Tales of Suspense with Iron Man*, and *Journey into Mystery with the Mighty Thor*.

Epic

The Epic series was created by Marvel Comics to highlight more adult-oriented themes and to provide comic book creators with more creative control over their work. Hints of an Epic line of books were being disclosed in 1979. It was billed as one of the most significant achievements since *Fantastic Four #1*. It has brought dozens of excellent projects to fruition that might otherwise have been passed up.

Epic 1 – The Magazine
Marvel Comics
Contains several note worthy
stories including an original
Silver Surfer tale.

Dreadstar #1
Marvel Comics
Jim Starlin's new series.
Went to First Comics after
its run at Epic.

Groo Graphic Novel
Marvel Comics
Another variation of the
Epic imprint (see top left
corner).

Other Marvel Imprints

Recent Marvel imprints include Max and Marvel Knights. Titles such as *Cage*, *Black Widow* and *Alias* are produced under the Max imprint. Titles such as *Elecktra* and *Captain America* are produced under the Marvel Knights imprint.

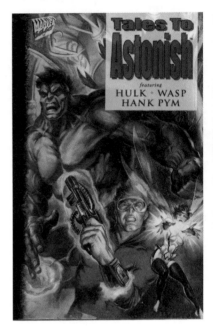

Tales to Astonish
Marvel Comics
Marvel Select – another publishing imprint – with a protective dust jacket.

Marvel Knights Daredevil
Marvel Comics
Gritty, adult storylines.

Justice League
DC Comics
Justice League of America 21.

Batman 17
DC Comics
Early Batman and Robin teamup.

DC Comics

Detective Comics or DC as the company would later be called is credited with creating the superhero genre in 1938 with the release of *Action Comics* #1 and what would become one of the most popular characters of all time – Superman. While Superman literally lives off light, the yellow sun's light, DC created another superhero that would complement and yet be a polar opposite. This is the dark knight – Batman. Together, these two superheroes define much of the fabric of the DC Universe.

Death of Superman
DC Comics
DC made the Death of Superman a media event, signaling the beginning of a grittier style of storytelling.

Amalgam *Magneto* #1
Amalgam Comics
Amalgam is an imprint of both DC and Marvel telling stories of superheroes that combine powers from both universes.

Other DC Imprints

DC also has some other imprints that focus on mainly adult or other types of experimental material. Two popular ones are *WildStorm* and *Vertigo*.

Dark Horse Comics

From the first appearance of Concrete to the issue of *Aliens #1* that became an instant collector's item, Dark Horse Comics has been showing us how to effectively compete in a crowded market place. Dark Horse is a major independent publisher that has not only survived, but has managed to prosper over

Aliens 2
Dark Horse Comics
Alien frontal portrait.

Aliens/Preditor #2
Dark Horse Comics
Chris Claremont's turn at Dark Horse.

the years by focusing on original properties, movie-related properties, tie-ins, and creator rights.

Dark Horse has had many successes including successful adaptations of *Aliens*, *Buffy the Vampire Slayer*, *Robocob*, and *The Terminator*. They have also been able to consistently publish strings of books from legendary creators such as John "Next Men" Byrne and Frank "Sin City" Miller.

Dark Horse is also a strong supporter of Manga and Anime. They are adapting the much-revered character *Astro-Boy*. Other Japanese adaptations include *Blade of the Immortal* and *Usagi Yojimbo*.

Black Cross 1
Dark Horse Comics
The violent tale of Black Cross.

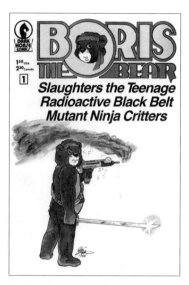

Boris the Bear #1
Dark Horse Comics
Cute animals become very popular
from time to time. Boris was
popular along with the Teenage
Mutant Ninja Turtles.

Flaming Carrot #18
Dark Horse Comics
Flaming Carrot series is a fan
favorite.

Dark Horse Aliens 1
Dark Horse Comics
Dark Horse has done a great *Aliens*
adaptation.

Image/Top Cow

Image Comics was founded by best selling artists who left established comic book publishers Marvel and DC. *Spawn* by Todd McFarlane was one of the first big money makers to emerge from Image. In addition to selling a gazillion comic books, it spawned a successful live action motion picture and lots of successful cartoons.

Gen 13 #1
Image
Poplular fan series.

Riptide #1
Image Comics
Nice legs. Good Liefeld art too.

Spawn 1
Image Comics
Spawn #1 by Todd
McFarlane. This is
the comic book
series that inspired
the hit movies.

Groo 1
Image Comics
Groo may win the
record for being
published by the
most publishers.

Rising Stars #2
Image Comics
Just about anything "Joe"
Straczynski writes is
worth reading!

Supreme #1
Image Comics
A new *Supreme* series.

Marvel *Micronauts* 1
Marvel
A pioneering series
based on action figure
toys.

PC Comics

In 1981, Pacific Comics (PC), named after a store on the Pacific coast, had the courage to compete head to head with the Big 2 – namely Marvel and DC. Their strategy was sound – hire some of the best talents in the industry, give them creative control, and distribute the masterpieces. They got the process right by hiring two of the most popular comic book creators in the marketplace. Jack "King" Kirby brought out *Captain Victory and the Galactic Rangers*. Mike Grell brought his own *Starslayer*.

***Starslayer* 1**
PC Comics
A beautiful wrap around painted cover.

Vanguard Illustrated #2
Pacific Comics
By Dave Stevens of
Rocketeer fame.

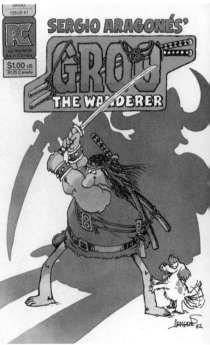

Pacific Groo 1
PC Comics
The second full Groo story.
Groo #1 from Eclipse was the
1st full Groo story.

Pacific Groo 2
PC Comics
Real life lesson: don't fall into
another problem while trying
to escape an existing one.

Western Publishing, Gold Key, & Whitman

Western Publishing began publishing *Mickey Mouse Magazine* in 1935. This started a long string of publications based on Walt Disney characters. In 1962, Western Publishing started publishing comics under the imprint of Gold Key Comics. Several characters were launched into their own books in the 1960s such as *Barks' Dagle Boys*, *Super Goof*, *Moby Duck* as well as a lot of science fiction and fantasy titles. For example, Gold Key launched the first *Star Trek* comic book adaptation. Western Publishing eventually stopped publishing under

X-Men #118 Whitman copy
Marvel Comics
A Whitman produced copy of the Marvel comic book.

X-Men #118 Regular copy
Marvel Comics
The original version of the Marvel comic book.

the Gold Key name and began to publish comic books under the Whitman name.

In the late 1970s and 1980s, Whitman entered into an agreement with Marvel to distribute their comics under the Whitman imprint. These are identical to the Marvel prints except that the bar code box is usually left completely blank (instead of containing a bar code or a Marvel character). For a long time the Whitman copies were considered to be reprints, however since the imprint has dropped out of sight in the last decade, many readers view both the Marvel and the Whitman versions as originals.

DELL

This publisher was a major player in the comic book industry in the 1960s and 1970s with some classic comic book titles that included *Tarzan*, *Dell 4-color series*, *Animal Comics*, *Bewitched*, *The Lost World* (1960-61), *The Untouchables* (1961-62) and *Lone Ranger's Companion Tonto* (1951-59) to name but a few. DELL comics in high grade continue to be blue chip investments, especially the ones with photo covers.

Get Smart 1
Gold Key
Photo cover from the popular 1960s spy spoof television series.

Flying Saucers
Dell
A Good minus (-) copy of *Flying Saucers Comics*.

Other Comic Book Publishers

Due to space limitations we cannot evaluate all the comic book publishers both past and present to the same level of detail. However, here are some of the publishers that have produced books that have actively been collected by fans at one time or another:

Archie; Aardvark-Vanaheim; Acclaim; Adventure; Atlas; Bongo Comics; Broadway Comics: Caliber Comics; Cartoon books; Centaur Publication; Chaos! Charlton Comics; Comico; Continuity Comics; CrossGeneration Comics; Defiant; E.C.; Eclipse Comics; Fantagraphics; Fawcett Publications; First Comics; Gladstone Publishing; Harris Comics/Warren; Harvey Comics; Innovation Publishing; Insight Studios Group; Kitchen Sink; Malibu; Maximum Press; Mirage Studios; Now; Oni Press; Russ Cochran/Gemstone Publishing; Sirius Comics; Topps Company; Valiant.

Deathmate
Valiant and Image
A publishing company cross-over.

Plasm
Defiant
Flagship title from Jim Shooter's post-Valiant efforts.

Justice Machine 1
Comico
Comico introduced the
industry to enhanced
and vibrant colors.

Kamui
Eclipse and Viz Comics
Came on the edge of a wave
of philosophical and martial
arts books

Green Hornet 1
NOW Comics
Solid adaptation of the 1960s
television series.

Flintstones
Gold Key
As cutting edge as the
Simpsons in their own
time.

Archie Comics
Archie Comics
Many people have wondered
how these characters remain so
popular, but they do.

Ghostly Haunts
Charlton Comics
Many Charlton Comic series are
being adapted by contemporary
comic book publishers.

Chapter 7:

What Fans Collect

Collecting was fairly simple at one time. First issues went up. Neal Adams art went up. Silver Surfer appearances went up. However, *X-Men* #94 changed all that. It was none of those things, yet it went up to $50 retail around 1979 and has gone up steadily since then. This section examines what fans collect.

What's In A Number?

Comic books are identified by a volume and an issue number. Certain issue numbers are sought after by their very nature. For example, consider the following.

First Issues

Collectors like to collect unique, original and rare items. For a long time, first issues (#1s) were rarely published in the industry. This made them rare and much sought after. This trend has continued and fans like to collect the first issue of a series.

Nova 1
Marvel Comics
Breakout
superhero of the
1970s.

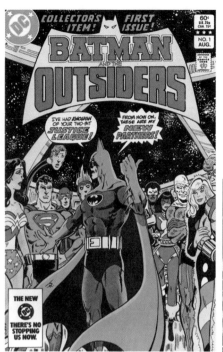

Batman and the Outsiders 1
DC Comics
Batman and the Outsiders #1.

Dazzler 1
Marvel Comics
From the pages of the *X-Men*,
the Dazzler gets her own
series.

Eternals 1
Marvel Comics
Another solid Kirby creation.

Elusive #2's

Something interesting started to happen in the comic book industry. Store owners started to anticipate the demand for #1s and would order several times the normal stock levels. They would then under order #2s. Publishers started to anticipate the surge in demand for number #1s and started printing more copies. Publishers would also underprint #2s. As collectors started realizing the rarity of #2s, they started snatching them up as well.

Creative Contributors

Collectors often focus on buying up all or most of the major work

Marvel *Fanfare* 2
Marvel Comics
Vastly under-ordered book by dealers.

Wolverine 2
Marvel Comics
Issue 1 reportedly sold 600,000 copies. #2 was under-ordered.

done by different creative contributors. Comic book art is the most sought after creative element by collectors. Finished comic book art is composed through a multi-step process that involves work from a penciller, inker and colorist.

Writers, of course, also play an important role in creating comic books. However, they have traditionally not been sought out with the same passion as the artist. This is changing though, as it has become obvious that strong plotting, storyline, and dialogue ultimately affect the quality and longevity of a storyline.

Wonder Woman #103
DC Comics
A John Byrne cover.

Ronin Book One
A Frank Miller cover.

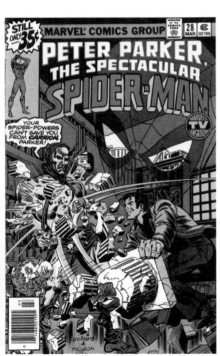

Spectacular Spider-Man #28
Marvel Comics
Keith Pollard pencils.

The Nam #1
Marvel Comics
Michael Goldon draws a
history of the Vietnam war.

**The Legion of Super-Heroes
#287**
DC Comics
Giffen's first work on a main
Legion of Super-Heroes story.

New Gods #1
DC Comics
A Jack Kirby cover.

The Twilight Zone
Now Comics
Neal Adams cover art.

Classic X-Men #1
Marvel Comics
Art Adams cover.

Guest Appearances and Cross-Overs

Guest appearances occur when a character appears in another title. This is very popular with comic book fans that may want to collect every appearance of their favorite character. In fact, there was a time that including a Silver Surfer appearance would instantly make a book successful and sought after by collectors.

Another much sought after derivation of the guest appearance is when two characters with a lot of mutual chemistry continue to appear together repeatedly. There is usually something in the match up that rivets readers. This could be a contrast in personalities, cultures, age groups, or powers.

The *X-Men* #35
Marvel Comics
Guest appearance by
Spider-Man.

Wonder Woman #287
DC Comics
Guest appearance by the New Teen
Titans.

Marvel Comics #8
First battle between the *Golden Age
Human Torch* and *Sub-Mariner.*

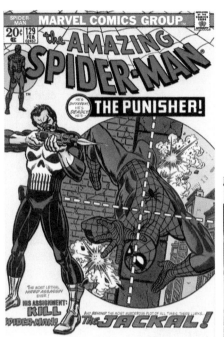

Spider-Man 129
Marvel Comics
1st apparance of the
Punisher!

Spider-Woman #20
Marvel Comics
Spider-Man really gets
around.

Fantastic Four 112
Marvel Comics
The Hulk versus the
Thing is a classic contest.

X-Men VS Teen Titans
DC and Marvel
A teamup everyone wanted to see in the 1980s.

Publishing Company Cross-Overs

The popularity of cross-overs and guest appearances was demonstrated early on as far back as the Golden Age. Popular pairings included Superman/Batman and Submariner/Human Torch. However, fans wanted more. They wanted cross publishing house pairings. Why not pair up the strongest DC superhero with the strongest Marvel superhero. How would they get along? Who would win in a battle? Would they cooperate with each other?

Initially there were many legal ramifications that were essentially showstoppers. Eventually, the comic book publishers (especially when

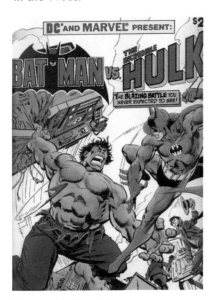

Batman VS Hulk
DC and Marvel
Bat-Soup anyone?

Spider-Man and Batman
DC and Marvel
Both heroes have dark backgrounds.

**Predator VS Magnus
Robot Fighter**
Dark Horse and Valiant
Valiant adapted the Gold
Key version of Magnus
Robot Fighter.

TMNT and Cerebus
Mirage Studios
Cerebus stars with the Teenage
Mutant Ninja Turtles.

**Green Lantern and the
Silver Surfer**
DC and Marvel
Cross company teamup starring
the Green Lantern and the
Silver Surfer.

creative people kept going back and forth between them anyway) relented and started to offer special projects that offered the pairings, usually with a lot of fanfare. One of the best early achievements was the 1970s pairing between Superman and Spider-Man. The next really successful one was the X-Men and the New Teen Titans.

One-Shots

Comic books have traditionally been published on a monthly schedule, i.e. 1 issue per month. Other schedules are also used including bimonthly, twice a year, annually, and even biweekly or weekly from time to time.

Another interesting derivation to the publishing schedule is the one shot story that has proven to be extremely popular with fans. This is essentially a comic book story that is self contained in a single, often double sized, issue. This offers a creative opportunity to tell a creative story, but to move it out of the usual continuity of a regular series.

Silver Surfer V2 #1
Marvel Comics
A much anticipated one shot story of the Silver Surfer by John Byrne (oh and Stan Lee).

Batman and Punisher
DC and Marvel
Both characters created out of tragedy are a natural partnership despite being the properties of different publishers.

One Shot – *Return of the Jedi*
Marvel Comics
Movie adaptations are common
sources for one shot stories.

One shot – *What If* 1
Marvel Comics
What If is a series of one-shot
stories that reflect on "what could
have been."

One shot – *FF Roast*
Marvel Comics
A takeoff on the Dean Martin
Celebrity roasts with the World's
Greatest as the guest of honors.

One shot – *Spider-Man and Daredevil*
Marvel Comics
Another classic teamup.

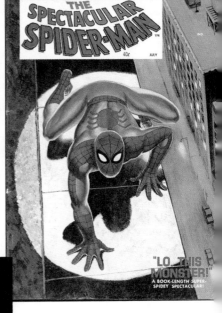

The Spectacular Spider-Man
Marvel Comics
Special first of a two part story.

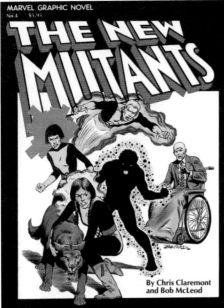

New Mutants Graphic Novel
Marvel Comics
1st appearance of the New Mutants as a one shot story before getting their own series.

COVERS

The cover of a comic book often sells the book. Some estimates, in fact, say that as much as 50% of purchases are made based on how the buyer responds to a cover. This fact has not been lost on comic book publishers who have gone from fairly basic covers predating the Silver Age to some really complex creations today.

Photo Covers

Photo covers sell books. Photo covers from the Golden and the Silver Age are hot and will continue to be blue chip investments in high grade. Some examples are Four Color Comics, Movie, Movie Comics, and Movie Classics. Nothing captures a piece of history quite like a photo cover. Some collectors collect history through these photo covers.

Photo Cover: *Married with Children #2*
Now Comics
Kelly Bundy from the hit television series.

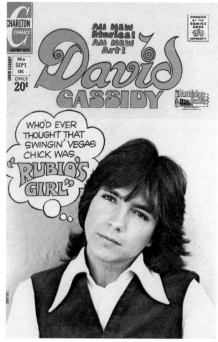

Photo Cover: David Cassidy
Charlton Comics
Legendary heart throb Keith from the *Partridge Family* played by David Cassidy.

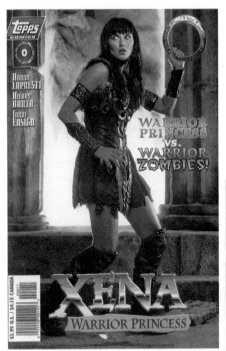

Photo Cover: *Xena* 0
Topps Comics
Based on the television series.

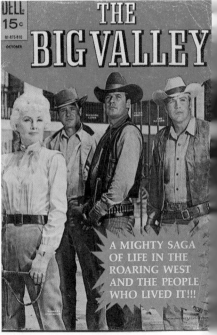

Photo Cover: *The Big Valley*
Dell
A *Big Valley* photo cover.

Photo Cover: *The Amazing Spider-Man* #262
Marvel Comics
Kind of looks like Tobey Maguire from the side.

Photo Cover: *The Rifleman*
Dell
Photo cover from the1950s hit
television series.

**Photo Cover: Roy Rogers
Comics**
Dell
Photo cover of Roy Rogers.

Photo Cover: *Bonanza*
Gold Key
Photo cover from *Bonanza*.

Cover Content

Cover content also has its own fans. This refers to the information that is included on the comic book cover. Some popular topics include action, sadness/melancholy, romance, provocative, suspenseful, bondage, portrait, and special content.

Marvel Premiere 50
Marvel Comics
1st rock and roll star
appearance/collaboration starring
Alice Cooper.

Primus
Charlton Comics
Suggestive, bondage cover.

Bondage Cover: *Spider-Woman*
Marvel Comics
Our money is on Spider-Woman
winning the fight.

Nova 12
Marvel Comics
A contrived story to get two superheroes to fight for a time. Usually ends in a draw.

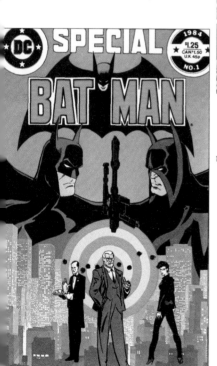

Contest of Champions 1
Marvel Comics
Something for just about everyone.

Batman Special #1
DC Comics
Classic stories of competing opposites.

Bizarre Adventures #27
Marvel Comics
Good exploration of the secret
lives of our favorite superheroes.

Marvel Premiere #57
Marvel Comics
1st Doctor Who comic book
adaptation in North America. Based
on the Tom Baker incarnation.

Fantastic Four 100
Marvel Comics
Special numeric milestones like 50,
100, 150, 200, etc are popular
collector's items.

Specially Constructed Covers

The direct sales market has led to a market that supports specially constructed covers. These can get quite complex and alluring, including the following:

- Baxter paper: heavy, extra white paper
- Die cut: print cut designs are on the cover made during the printing process
- Hologram: cover has a hologram affixed to it
- Gatefold: more than one folded over cover
- Foil: metallic foil on cover
- Flicker: images on the cover appear to move when the book is moved
- Chromium: foil of this type used on a cover
- Embossed: some area of the cover is raised
- Painted: cover is made from a painting
- Wrap around: The cover extends on both the front and the back of the book
- Infinity: Image on the cover contains increasing smaller versions of the same image creating an interesting "time-travel" type effect
- Bondage: an image of people, usually attractive women, restrained in some way.

Marvel Fanfare 1
Marvel Comics
Started a trend in the use of expensive glossy paper.

Camelot 3000 #1
DC Comics
Printed on durable Baxter paper.

Silver Surfer 50
Marvel Comics
Raised cover image.

Wonder Woman 1
DC Comics
Wraparound Perez cover that rumor says caused an editor
to hug George Perez.

Reprints

Reprints are a great way to read and experience comics that you normally could not afford to buy, or you might have a graded comic that you can't read because it is sealed in plastic.

Can you spot the physical difference between the two *Star Wars* covers? They are almost identical except for the small vertical strip labeled "reprint" in the second cover. Other covers may be indistinguishable, but the inside cover may contain a reprint statement. Before jumping at a bargain, establish whether the issue you are buying is a reprint or an original.

Marvel *Star Wars* V1#1:
Marvel Comics
1st comic book adaptation of the superhit movie.

Marvel *Star Wars* V1#1 Reprint:
Marvel Comics
Can you tell if this is a reprint? There is a stamp in the top left corner.

X-Men 1
Marvel Comics
Reprint of the original
comic book.

FF Galactus Trilogy
Marvel Comics
Reprint of the classic
Galactus story in tabloid
format.

A more sophisticated version of the reprint occurs when you buy a great story that has great art and is clearly labeled Volume 1 #1 with absolutely no "reprint" tags whatsoever. The problem here is that the entire story is actually reprinted from another series, but under a new name.

Chapter 8:
Where to Buy and Sell Comic Books

any of us hear from a friend about a neighbor or relative who happened to be a regular comic book collector in the early to late 1960s. They picked up good runs of books from classic series like the *Amazing Spider-Man*, *Fantastic Four*, *Tales to Astonish*, *Tales of Suspense*, *Journey into Mystery*, *X-Men*, *Submariner*, *Action*, *Detective*, *Legion of Superheroes*, the occasional Dell, and a few *Mads* or *National Lampoons*. In some cases the collections started at #1 or the beginning of a series, and sometimes there were two or three copies of the occasional rare comic that the person bought in error. To top it off, this contact was willing to part with the collection if it went to some kid who would continue the hobby. For the rest of us, building up a collection is a much more time consuming and difficult process.

Where to Buy Comic Books

In the early days of comics, there was only one place to buy them – the corner store. Comic book readers or collectors would have to time their visits to the corner stores just right, in order to be able to grab the copy or two of the series that they wanted to collect. If they arrived too late and

someone else bought the copies, it was too bad.

Specialty Stores

These are stores that specialize in selling comic related items, including, of course comic books. Most major cities have several of these stores. As per the 10 survival rules, a collector should build a relationship with at least one reliable dealer. You can preorder most of the books you want, get a discount, and ensure that you don't miss any more issues in the future.

Conventions

Comic book fandom hosts a lot of conventions in major cities across the world each year. These offer a good opportunity to find good deals on hot books and hard too find books. Comic book creators and editors also attend conventions, so they offer a good opportunity to get professional contacts.

Mail Order

If dealers and conventions are not near you, it is always possible to order your comic books through the mail. Most of the comic book publishers offer this service. There are also third party services that will mail the books to you – often at a discount. However, look at the total price you are asked to pay including shipping and handling. This may eat up your discount.

A key problem with mail order is the subscription crease or other damage done to a comic book through the mailing process. Before getting a subscription, get the assurance that your books will be sent in protective containers that will let them arrive in Mint or Near Mint condition.

Online Auctions

The Internet has had a profound impact on comic book collecting. Online auctions allow collectors to have an opportunity to find really hard to find items and to potentially get them at a really good price. eBay™, of course, is one of the largest auction sites. However, Amazon and other websites also offer comic book auctions and sales.

Here are some strategies for doing well on Internet auctions.

- Try to find a book online a day or so before the auction is over
- Get into serious bidding for an item about a minute or so before the auction is over
- Try to find a few instances of the same item and focus on the one that has the fewest bidders
- Abandon bidding on an item that has too many buyers willing to bid the price up to much

Here are some other considerations for Internet auctions.

- Check feedback before entering into a transaction with anyone
- Shipping costs can significantly impact the actual price you pay for a purchase. I once won an auction with a $60 bid on 2000 comic books or 3¢ a book. By the time the collection arrived, there was a $250 shipping charge on top of the auction price, raising the effective price per book to nearly 16¢ a book.
- Never send cash in the mail.
- Do NOT bid what you cannot afford to spend. An online auction is binding.
- Maintain restraint when bidding online. Don't try to win at any cost.
- Never make bidding personal.

Corner Store

You can still buy comic books at the corner store.

Where to Sell Comic Books

There are many reasons people sell comics. Ideally, they are being sold at a profit. There are many reasons why comic books go up in value.

- Ultimate representation of capitalism, supply & demand economics.
- Comics that are purchased for collections are taken off the market for many years.

- Comic books are fragile. Many comic buyers read the books, then discard them, rip them, leave them in the rain, or fold them.
- Characters, artists, or writers get hot.
- Childhood memories.
- Motion picture tie-in.
- Speculators and investors can drive demand as long as they remain interested.
- People don't always buy an issue when it first comes out.
- Older comic books used cheaper paper so many of the older comic books are in bad shape. Newer books use a better quality paper so the books will last a lot longer in higher grades.

For the most part, selling outlets are the same as the buying outlets except maybe for the corner store and some of the subscription options. Price your books according to condition based on information in price guides. Do not expect to get a dealer to pay the same for your books as his/her selling price. They are operating a business and have other overheads that have to be paid out of their profits. However, you should insist that they grade your books using the same criteria as the books they are selling. You may want to visit a comic shop before selling and build familiarity with their grading approach. Don't let him or her know you plan on selling.

Try not to let anyone cherry pick your comic book collection. This means selling your best stuff for perhaps a good price, but leaving marginal stuff behind in the collection. It will be difficult to get more than a dime or so for each of the remaining comic books.

Sell comics when they are in demand. Most are at one time or another. Enjoy your collection. In time most books get their turn in the limelight. There are not too many worthless 10¢ and 12¢ comics out there.

How to Know When You're Being Ripped Off

Most of us don't have a spider-sense so here are some things to watch out for when you're buying or selling comic books.

- Counterfeit books
- Books missing coupons inside – especially a problem for books from the 1960s and 1970s.
- Pre-1980 annuals were large books that are hard to find in near-mint or better condition because of generally broken or torn spines.
- Cover/inside conditions not consistent.
- Mail order – not getting what you paid for.
- Are you buying a reprint without realizing it?

Chapter 9:

How Much to Pay for a Comic Book – Making the Grade

There are many factors that go into how much a comic book is worth - at the top of the list is how badly someone wants to own it. Fortunately, there is a more objective process for determining a comic book's price or value. The price that collectors are willing to pay for a comic book is generally based on three factors.

- The comic book's title and issue number, which uniquely identifies it.
- The current physical condition of the comic book.
- How much a buyer is prepared to pay for the book.

Of these, the first piece of information is on the cover or inside the comic book. Using this unique key, you can locate the comic book(s) in a price guide. This gives you a range of prices that the book(s) could be worth. Now comes the difficult part. You need to determine what the grade or condition of the book is. If the book has been graded by an official third party, you only need to decide whether you believe the grade. However, if a grade has not been assigned, you and the other party need to agree on what it should be.

Grading Comic Books

Grading a comic book is the act of evaluating its physical condition. The grade of a comic book is not static. It will never go up by natural means, but it can degrade over time. Establishing a grade at any point in time is an assessment of the number and types of defects that a particular book has which would keep it from being an off the press copy.

The tables on pages 106-107 contains the grades that are commonly used to assess the physical condition of a comic book.

The following table shows how the numbers between 1 and 10.0 can also be used to map to the alphanumeric based scale.

9.9-10	Mint
9.8	NM-Mint
9.6	NM+
9.4	NM
9.2	NM-
9.0	VF-NM
8.5	VF+
8.0	VF
7.5	VF-

7.0	F-VF
6.5	F+
6.0	F
5.5	F-
5.0	VG-F
4.5	VG+
4.0	VG
3.5	VG-
3.0	G-VG
2.5	G+
2.0	G
1.5	Fair-Good
1.0	Fair
.5	Poor

Some collectors use the '+' or '-' as exponents to indicate that the grading is in between the firm conditions. For example, NM- is a condition between Near Mint and Fine.

Defects and Flaws

Here are some of the common defects or flaws that can afflict a comic book. Their penalty impact on a grade can be described as (1) severe – full grade; (2) major – ½ grade; (3) minor – depends on the number and extent of the damage.

- Stress lines: can occur anywhere on a comic book spine especially around the staples [minor defect].
- Store/date stamps: date a comic book shipment was received at a store, usually done by a clerk on the top copy of a shipment [no grade impact].
- Rolled spine: caused by folded pages [major defect].
- Subscription crease: a vertical crease down the length of a comic book caused by folding, handling in the subscription process [severe defect].
- Page color: yellow, brown, or brittle colored paper [severe defect].
- Missing coupon: some publishers in the 1970s included coupons for prizes or merchandize ordering. Some of these have been clipped [major defect].
- Loose cover: some or all portions of a cover are becoming detached from the comic book [severe defect].
- Water damaged [severe defect].
- Printing defects: off-center cover, miscut pages, bad page trimming, bad stapling, faded color, other typographical errors, wrinkling [depends].
- Flaking: small circles of a cover are chipped away, usually around the staples or edges [minor to major defects].
- Coverless: missing most or all of the book's cover [severe defect].

When assessing the grade of a comic book, consider that there are some offsetting factors. Older books will naturally have some page yellowing, for example.

	Mint (M)	Near Mint (NM)	Fine (F)
Overall appearance	Newstand copy	Must be complete	Minor wear is visible
Printing defects	None	None	None
Bindery defects	None	None	None
Cover flatness	Completely	Completely	Completely
Cover surface wear	None	None	Minor
Cover brightness	Bright	Bright	Some dull
Cover centering	Centered	Centered	Centered
Staples	Clean, no rust	Clean, no rust	Dulling
Color fading	None	None	Slight
Soiling	None	None	None
Staining	None	None	None
Discoloration	None	None	None
Acidity	None visible	None visible	Slight
Page color	Brilliant, White	Brilliant, White	White
Rips/tears	None	None	None
Stress lines/ wrinkles	None	Some stress lines	1 or 2 wrinkles
Missing pages/ coupons	None	None	None
Severe Defects	None	None	None
Other	Prized condition	Prized condition	Very collectable

	Very Good (VG)	Good (G)	Fair (Fr)	Poor (P)
Overall appearance	Wrinkling	Tolerable	Not pleasing	Not pleasing
Printing defects	1 or 2	More than 2	More than 2	More than 2
Bindery defects	Loose page	Loose pages	Lots	Lots
Cover flatness	Slight page warping	Page warping	Pages warped	Pages warped
Cover surface wear	Some	Lots of wear	Lots of wear	Lots of wear
Cover brightness	Dull in places	Dull	Dull	Very Dull
Cover centering	Slight off centering	Off center	Off center	Very off center
Staples	Misaligned	Misaligned, rusting	Loose, rusted	Loose, rusted
Color fading	Minor	Lots	Lots	Lots
Soiling	Slight	Minor	Lots	Lots
Staining	Slight	Minor	Lots	Lots
Discoloration	Slight	Minor	Lots	Lots
Acidity	Minor	Lots	Lots	Lots
Page color	Some yellowing	Yellowing	Browning	Browning
Rips/tears	1 or 2 small ones	More than 2	More than 3	More than 3
Stress lines/ wrinkles	Some wrinkles and stress lines	Lots of wrinkles and stress lines	Many	Many
Missing pages/ coupons	None	Small coupon missing	Coupons missing	Coupons missing
Severe Defects	None	Yes	Yes	Yes
Other	Affordable	Reading copy	Reading copy	Readying copy

Grading Examples
Here are some comic book covers with the grades that can be assigned to them based on an examination of the cover. The contents of the book would need to be in similar condition for the grade to hold:

Mint Condition – *Spectacular Spider-Man* 200
Marvel Comics
Flawless comic. Great colors, no wrinkles, and full cover gloss.

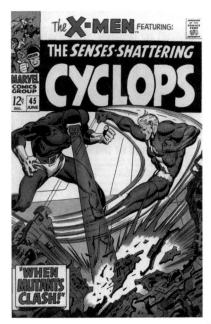

Near Mint Condition – *X-Men* 121
Marvel Comics
No visible defects.

Very Fine Condition – *X-Men* 45
Marvel Comics
Based on the age of the comic book, there are vibrant colors, no tears, and tight spine. Beautiful copy.

Fine Condition – *The Spectacular Spider-Man* #220
Marvel Comics
The staples are in a little too deep. One tiny smudge in bottom left corner.

Very Good – *Dennis the Menace* #101
Fawcett
Small crease in top right corner, cover fading.

Good Condition – *Green Lantern* #23
DC Comics
We'd put this one just under Good, but have bumped it up due to its age.

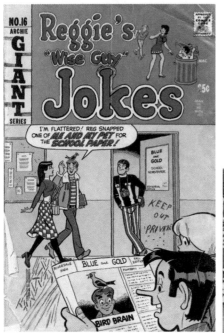

Poor Condition
Archie Comics
Well read copy.

Subscription Crease – *X-Men* #4
Marvel Comics
Vertical creases are usually caused by folding the book over onto itself or sending it through the mail.

Coverless Comic – *Mystery 3*
Marvel Comics
A coverless copy of *Marvel Mystery* #3.

Coupon Example
Marvel Comics
Look for missing coupons anywhere in a comic book.

Back Cover
Marvel Comics
Examine the back cover because it reflects the handling a comic book has received.

One approach to remove the ambiguity from having two parties grade a comic book is to involve a third independent party to establish strict grading guidelines and to certify the results. This is the principle behind the Comics Guaranty Corporation (CGC) or Comics Guaranty, LLC. This organization will do the following for you:

- Receive your comic book(s)
- Analyze the condition of the comic book(s)
- Assign grade(s) on an individual basis and make them highly visible
- Seal the book in a plastic sleeve or inner "well". The sleeve is not airtight.
- Some treated paper is inserted at points in the comic book to help protect it and to absorb other harmful contaminants

The third party evaluators should take special care when examining the books, such as wearing gloves and using flat surfaces. In return for the grading service, the collector pays a monetary fee to the third party. This correspondingly tends to increase the value of the comic book that is certified. At present, there is a high demand for high quality books that have been graded by the CGC that easily sell at many times the price listed in standard price guides. However, the basis for this is currently an under supply of third party graded comic books especially in high grades. When paying a price unlisted in any of the industry's main price guides, be sure you want the book itself. There is no guarantee the price you paid on the Internet can be reclaimed later.

The front of the CGC graded comic book has some useful information that can be read at a glance.

- Rating: shown clearly on a printed color strip, as both an alphanumeric and decimal grade.
- Top Left Corner Colored Strip: this is used to further elaborate on the grade with an indication of any other factors of which a collector should become aware. Yellow – Signature Series; Purple – book is restored; Green – serious qualified defect in the book; Blue – Universal.
- Bar Code: this is unique for every CGC book and can be used to certify the authenticity of a graded copy. These can be communicated to the organization for additional information on the comic book.
- Official CGC hologram in the top right corner

The sealed comic is stored in a CGC protective collar that further protects the book from being manipulated. The book is sealed in place in this collar. Removal of the book or tampering will break the corners of the case and potentially nullify the rating because a third party was not the last to handle it.

CGC is backed by several industry players, providing it with another level of support, including Wizard, Topcow, Dynamic Forces, and Chaos! The website address is www.CGCcomics.com.

To Officially Grade or Not

Graded books are intended to be investments as they can no longer be handled or read. Our advice is to be reasonable in selecting the number of comics you want to get certified. Be careful not to get carried away and pay too much for high-grade comics which are just like stocks in many ways. There's always a peak. Just look at some of the "for sure" stocks that have crashed, although we don't believe comics are exactly like stocks where the company's performance affects price. They can still go down in value especially for newer comics in the last say 20 some odd years. As more comics get graded and more 9.4 –10.0s pop up, the price will start to drop.

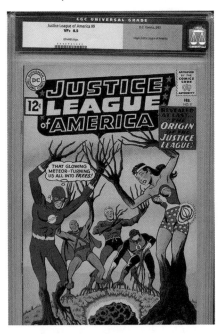

CGC Graded Book: JLA VF+ 8.5
DC Comics
A CGC graded comic book bought over the Internet.

Circulation

The number of copies in existence of a key comic book determines its value and appreciation potential. As the saying goes, "there is only so much water front property available in the world." Similarly, there are only a limited number of high-grade comic books available in the world. If you're talking about the Golden Age, this number is very small. With the poor quality of paper that was used before the Modern Age, high-grade books from those eras will be increasingly difficult to find. Post 1980 books used better stock paper so these should be more readily available.

There are some hot books after 1980 that have held onto their price increase, but which are not actually in short supply. It is rumored that over 1 million copies of *Spider-Man* #1 by Todd McFarlane were sold. The paid circulation for books published in the period 1995-2000 is considered to be low. There is a potential that these will get very high in demand some point in the future.

Most regular series publish their circulation numbers once a year in a book. The information is presented in terms of total print run, free copies circulated, and sold copies. This information is audited and used to justify advertising and other revenue.

***X-Men* #156**
Marvel Comics
This issue contains a Statement of Circulation on the letters page.

***The Amazing Spider-Man* #298**
Marvel Comics
1st McFarlane Spider-Man art.

Chapter 10:
Protecting Your Collection

Other hobbies also have fragile collectibles. Porcelain figures break, silverware gets tarnished, coins get scratched, and stamps get damaged. So what makes comic books so special in terms of the need to protect them? Their enjoyment comes from being handled repeatedly, whereas many other collectibles can be put into a glass container and enjoyed from a distance. True enjoyment with comic book collections comes from looking at the covers now and then, and occasionally to go through an old collection and bring out a book and read it from cover to cover. It's difficult to identify another hobby that involves handling such fragile merchandise so frequently.

Common Dangers	
Activity	**Hazard**
Buying	Bending, ripping, folding
Reading	Folding the pages back when reading them Spilling a liquid on top of the comic book
Piling	Crushing books at the bottom of a pile Putting unbagged copies underneath bagged copies and tape gets stuck to the unbagged covers
Archiving	Putting unbagged comics against bagged ones that have tape which attaches to the unbagged comic
General Hazards	Light, moisture, heat

Protective Gear
Protecting a comic book collection involves several separate activities:
- Proper and gentle handling when the comic books are being browsed or read
- Proper and safe storage
- Insurance for very expensive books

Safe Handling

Handle a comic book like you would handle a baby. No fast moves. Turn the pages gently without grabbing too tightly. Use very clean hands. Hold the book flat while you are reading it.

Proper and Safe Storage

Safe and proper storage of a comic book means the following activities:

- Comic books should be individually bagged in virgin polyethylene/polypropylene plastic or Mylar Type "D" sleeves. Mylar is more expensive, but it is also more effective in eliminating acid from the pages of the comic book. The bags should be replaced on a regular basis (as per instructions from the manufacturer). A guideline of one a year is a good place to start.
- Each comic can get extra protection by getting backed by an acid-free board, which is then put inside the plastic bag with the book. The back board protects against the book being bent and it also absorbs acid from the pages of the comic book.
- The protected comic book should be stored in a cardboard box specifically sized to hold comic books. Don't force the comics in too tight, and don't leave too much empty space. The books should fit comfortably in the cardboard boxes without getting bashed around if the box is moved.

The cardboard boxes should be stored in a cool, dark and dry place. A constant temperature of 68°F is ideal. The storage location should have a low humidity. The storage location should ideally be in a separate room, certainly away from traffic, kids, and pets. There should be no direct light on the books. The storage location should also be free of insects and protected against a change in the elements (e.g. flooding, water leakage).

Standard Polyethylene Bag
Marvel Comics
Polyethylene bag and backboard offer basic protection for a comic book.

Deacidified Bag
Marvel Comics
Deacidified envelope offers more protection than the polyethylene bag.

Mylar Sleeve
Marvel Comics
Deacidified comic sleeve, bag, and backboard. This is a well-protected comic book.

Superman white encased
DC Comics
Comic comes sealed directly from the publisher.

Comic Book Insurance

Insurance against common hazards should be considered. It tends to be expensive when you're talking about a lot of books, but if you have a couple of key, expensive books, it might be something you want to do. You should also find out if your collection or some portion of it is insured under any homeowner's policy that you might have.

Restoration

Restoration work is used to improve the appearance of a comic book that is heavily damaged. It always requires a professional or a comic book doctor. Never, ever try to restore a comic book yourself. You will damage it permanently.

All books are candidates for restoration, however, practically speaking, only valuable books have a return on investment (ROI) that makes them suitable for the process. You will be charged a fee for the restoration work so the process must add enough value to the restored comic to make the fee and the time spent justifiable. In general, books that are worth more than $250 in restored condition can be considered as candidates.

Since restoration work improves the appearance of a comic book, it must be disclosed to prospective buyers of the book. A restored book has a lower grade than the same issue that has never been restored.

There are two types of restoration. The first involves structural work, while the second involves image improvements. Structural work is simpler and less invasive of the two. The restoration process involves a combination of the following activities:

- Color touch up
- Paper repair
- Replacing missing pages
- Re-glossing
- Cleaning
    Dry
    Chemical
    Water
- Removal of external objects
    Tape
- Removal of spine roll
- Deacidification
- Bleaching
- Trimming

Chapter 11:

Lists for Collectors

Collectors in all hobbies tend to like lists. The comic book hobby is no different. Lists can be used to build a historical path down memory lane.

Artists

Here is a list of well-known and collected artists. There are many, many other artists out there who we can't list due to space limitations. An abbreviation for the artist is shown in brackets after the name:

Adams, Art (aadams); Adams, Neal (nadams); Aparo, Jim (japaro); Aragones, Sergio (saragone); Bagley, Mark (Mbagley); Baker, Matt (Mbaker); Barks, Carl (Cbarks); Beck, C.C. (cbeck); Bolland, Brian (bbolan); Broderick, Pat (Pbrode); Brunner, Frank (Fbrunr); Buardineer, Fred (fbuard); Buscema, John (Jbusc); Byrne, John (Jbyr); Campbell, J. Scott (scamp); Chadwick, Paul (Pchad); Chaykin, Howard (Hchay); Cole, L.B. (lcole); Craig, Johnny (Jcraig); Crandall, Reed (rcrand); Gibbons, Dave (dgibb); Davis, Jack (jdavis); Disbrow, Jayson (Jdisbrw); Ditko, Steve (Sdit); Fisner, Will (Weisner); Elder, Bill (belder); Evans, George (Gevans); Everett, Bill (Bever); Feldstein, Al (afeld); Fine, Lou (lfine); Foster, Harold (hfostr); Fox, Matt (Mfox); Frazetta, Frank (Ffraz); Giffen, Keith (kgiff); Golden, Michael (mGold);

Gottfredson, Floyd (Fgott); Grell, Mike (MGrel); Guice, Butch (Bguice); Gustavson, Paul (Pgust); Heath, Russ (Rheath); Howard, Wayne (whowrd); Infantino, Carmen (cinfan); Ingels, Graham (gingls); Jones, Jeff (jjones); Jurgens, Dan (Djurgn); Kamen, Jack (jkamen); Kane, Bob (Bkane); Kane, Gil (Gkane); Kelly, Walt (Wkelly); Keown, Dale (Dkeown); Kieth, Sam (Skieth); Kinstler, E.R. (Ekinst); Kirby, Jack (Jkirby); Krenkel, Roy (rkren); Krigstein, Bernie (bkrig); Kubert, Adam & Andy (A&AKub); Kubert, Joe (Jkubrt); Kurtzman, Harvey (Hkurtz); Lapham, Dave (dlapham): Larsen, Erik (elrsen): Layton, Bob (Blayton); Lee, Jae (jaelee); Lee, Jim (jimlee); Liefeld, Rob (Rlief); Lim, Rom (RLim); Manning, Russ (Rmann): McFarlane, Todd (TMcfar); McWilliams, Al (Amcwil); Meskin, Mort (Mmesk); Mignola, Mike (Mmign); Miller, Frank (Miller); Moreira, Ruben (Rmorra); Morisi, Pete (Pmorisi); Newton, Don (dnewton); Nostrand, Howard (Hnostr); Orlando, Joe (jorland); Pakula, Mac (Mpak); Palais, Rudy (rpalais); Perez, George (Perez); Portacio, Whilce (Wport); Powell, Bob (Bpow); Quesada, Joe (jquesd); Raboy, Mac (mraboy); Ramos, Humberto (Hramos); Ravielli, Louis (Lravili); Raymond, Alex (Araym); Redondo, Nestor

(Nredon); Rogers, Marshall (Mrogers); Romita Jr, John (Jromjr); Ross, Alex (Aross); Sale, Tim (Tsale); Schomburg, Alex (Aschom); Sears, Bart (Bsears); Siegel & Shuster (Si&Sh); Sienkiewicz, Bill (bsien); Silvestri, Marc (Msil); Simonson, Walt (Wsim); Smith, Barry Windsor (BWS); Smith, Paul (Psm); Stanley, John (Jstan); Starlin, Jim (Jstarln); Staton, Joe (Jstatn); Steranko, Jim (Jster); Stevens, Dave (Dstev); Swan, Kurt (Kswan); Texeira, Mark (Tex); Thibert, Art (athibt); Thoth, Alex (Athoth); Torres, Angelo (Atorres); Tuska, George (gtuska); Ward, Bill (bward); Williamson, Al (Awill); Woggon, Bill (Bwogg); Wolverton, Basil (Bwolv); Wood, Wallace (WWood); Wrightson, Bernie (Bwri); Zeck, Mike (mzeck)

First Character Appearances

Here is a list of first appearances for popular characters. Prices are for copies in near mint+ (NM+) condition (or approximately 9.6 with the assumption that somewhere the book exists).

Using the prices for books not in NM+ or 9.6 condition (which is 100% of our pricing), use the following formula:

9.0 = 50% of our price listing
8.0 = 30% of our price listing
6.0 = 20% of our price listing
4.0 = 10% of our price listing
2.0 = 5% of our price listing

When cover price is greater than listed price, use the comic cover price.

Legend:
Numbers with (–) are consecutive
  1st = first appearance
  O = origin
  D = death
  Cameo = 2 pages or less
  GS = Giant Size

Adam Strange - *Showcase* #17 nov 1958 (DC) $4,200
Alicia Masters - *Fantastic Four* #8 nov 1962 (Marvel) $1,500
Alien Costume (Venom) - *Amazing Spider-Man* #252 may 1984 (Marvel) $40
All Star Squadron - *Justice League of America* #193 aug 1981 (DC) $5
Alpha Flight (Cameo) - *X-Men* #120 Apr 1978 (Marvel) $140
Alpha Flight (Full) - *X-Men* #121 may 1979 (Marvel) $160
Andy Panda - *Crackerjack Funnies* #39 sept 1941 (Dell) $750
Anthro - *Showcase* #74 may/68 (DC) $95
Ant-Man - *Tales to Astonish* #27 jan 1962 (Marvel) $6,000
Aqualad - *Adventure Comics* #269 feb 1960 (DC) $350
Aquaman (SA) - *Adventure Comics* #260 may 1959 (DC) $1,000
Aquaman - *More Fun Comics* #73 nov 1941 (DC) $18,000
Archie Andrews - *Pep Comics* #22 dec 1941 (MLJ Mag.) $21,000
Atom, The (GA) - *All-American Comics* #19 oct 1940 (DC)
                         $24,000
Aunt May - *Amazing Fantasy* #15 aug 1962 (Marvel) $58,000
Aurora - *X-Men* #120 (Marvel) $140
Avengers, The - *Avengers* #1 Sept 1963 (Marvel) $4,200

Baby Huey - *Casper, The Friendly Ghost* #1 sept 1949 (St. John Pub.) $2,100

Bat-Girl - *Batman* #139 apr 1961 (DC) $225

Bat-Mite - *Detective Comics* #267 may 1959 (DC) $450

Batarang - *Detective Comics* #31 sept 1939 (DC) $40,000

Batgirl (Barbara Gordon) - *Detective Comics* #359 jan 1967 (DC) $195

Batman, The - *Detective Comics* #27 may 1939 (DC) $325,000

Batplane - *Detective Comics* #31 sept 1939 (DC) $40,000

Batwoman - *Detective Comics* #233 jul 1956 (DC) $2,000

Beast, The (New) - *X-Men* #1 sept 1963 (Marvel) $14,000

Betty (Archie) - *Pep Comics* #22 dec 1941 (MLJ Mag.) $21,000

Bizarro - *Superboy* #68 oct 1956 (DC) $750

Black Bolt (Cameo) - *Fantastic Four* #45 dec 1965 (Marvel) $195

Black Bolt (full) - *Fantastic Four* #46 jan 1946 (Marvel) $140

Black Cat - *Amazing Spider-Man* #194 jul 1979 (Marvel) $25

Black Condor, The - *Crack Comics* #1 may 1940 (Quality Comics Group) $7,200

Black Flame - *Action Comics* #304 sept 1963 (DC) $65

Black Knight (new) - *Avengers* #48 jan 1968 (Marvel) $50

Black Orchid - *Adventure Comics* #428 jun 1973 (DC) $50

Black Panther (GA) - *Stars & Stripes Comics* #3 jul 1941 (CentaurPub.) $1,500

Black Panther (SA) - *Fantastic Four* #52 jul 1966 (Marvel) $250

Black Terror, The - *Exciting Comics* #9 may 1941 (Standard Comics) $12,500

Black Widow - *Mystic Comics* #4 jul 1940 (Timely Comics) $4,200

Black Widow (SA) - *Tales of Suspense* #52 april 1964 (Marvel) $250

Blackhawk - *Military Comics* #1 Aug 1941 (Quality Comics Group) $12,000

Blob, The - *X-Men* #3 jan 1964 (Marvel) $1,300

Blonde Phantom - *All-Select Comics* #11 fall 1946 (Timely Comics) $3,500

Blondie - *Ace Comics* #1 apr 1937 (David McKay Pub) $4,200

Bloodshot - *Eternal Warrior* (cameo) #4 nov 1992 (Valiant\Acclaim) $5

Blue Beetle, The - *Mystery Men Comics* #1 aug 1939 (Fox Features Syndicate) $15,000

Blue Bolt - *Blue Bolt* #1 jun 1940 (Novelty Press\Premium Group) $3,800

Blue Streak, The - *Crash Comics* #1 may 1940 (Tem Pub.) $4,000

Bomba - *Bomba, the Jungle Boy* #1 Sept 1967 (DC) $50

Bouncing Boy - *Action Comics* #276 may 1961 (DC) $250

Boy Commandos - *Detective Comics* #64 jun 1942 (DC) $5,000

Brainiac - *Action Comics* #242 jul 1958 (DC) $2,500

Brainiac 5 - *Action Comics* #276 may 1961 (DC) $250

Buck Rogers - *Famous Funnies* #3 sept 1934 (Eastern Color) $5,800

Bucky - *Captain America Comics* #1 mar 1941 (Marvel) $100,000

Bugs Bunny - *Looney Tunes & Merrie Melodies Comics* #1 1941 (Dell) $17,500

Bullet - *Daredevil* #250 dec 1988 (Marvel) $5

Bullseye - *Nick Fury Agent of Shield* #15 nov 1969 (Marvel) $195

Bullseye - *Nick Fury Agent of Shield* #15 nov 1969 (Marvel) $75

Bullseye (new) - *Daredevil* #131 (Marvel)**** $40

Cable (Cameo) - *New Mutants* #86 feb 1990 (Marvel) $15

Cable (Full) - *New Mutants* #87 mar 1990 (Marvel) $35

Cap'n Quick - *Eclipse Magazine* #1 may 1981 (Eclipse) $5

Capt. George Stacy - *Amazing Spider-Man* #56 jan 1968 (Marvel) $195

Captain America - *Captain America Comics* #1 mar 1941 (Marvel) $100,000

Captain America (silver age) - *Avengers* #4 mar 1964 (Marvel) $2,500

Captain Cold - *Showcase* - #8 may 1957 (DC) $16,000

Captain Marvel Jr. - *Whiz Comics* #25 dec 1941 (Fawcett Pub.) $7,500

Captain Marvel (Female) - *Amazing Spider-Man* Annual #16 1982 (Marvel) $10

Captain Marvel (Shazam) - *Whiz Comics* #1 feb 1940 (Fawcett) $125,000

Captain Midnight - *Funnies, The* #57 jul 1941 (Dell) $5,000

Captain Savage - *Mystery Men Comics* #4 nov 1939 (Fox Features) $3,000

Captain Storm - *Captain Storm* #1 May 1964 (DC) $95

Captain Victory - *Our Flag Comics* #1 aug 1941 (Ace Mag.) $3,000

Casper - *Casper, The Friendly Ghost* #1 sept 1949 (St. John Pub.) $2,100

Cat-Man (Villain) - *Detective Comics* #318 jan 1963 (DC) $95

Catman - *Crash Comics* #4 oct 1940 (Tem Pub.) $3,800

Catwoman (first with costume) - *Batman* #3 fall 1940 (DC) $12,500

Catwoman (no costume) - *Batman* #2 sum 1940 (DC) $19,500

Cave Carson - *Brave & the Bold* #31 aug 1960 (DC) $500

Cerebus - *Cerebus The Aardvark* #1 dec 1977 (Aardvark-Vanaheim) $300

Challengers of the Unknown - *Showcase* #6 jan 1957 (DC) $5,800

Chameleon - *Amazing Spider-Man* #1 mar 1963 (Marvel) $40,000

Chameleon Boy - *Action Comics* #267 aug 1960 (DC) $500

Champions - *Champions* #1 oct 1975 (Marvel) $25

Champions, The - *The Champions* #1 oct 1975 (Marvel) $40

Changeling - *X-Men* #35 aug 1967 (Marvel) $250

Changeling (Beast Boy) - *New Teen Titans* #1 nov 1980 (DC) $25

Clay Face - *Detective Comics* #40 jun 1940 (DC) $8,900

Clayface (Silver Age) - *Detective Comics* #298 dec 1961 (DC) $350

Cloak & Dagger - *Spectacular Spider-Man* #64 mar 1982 (Marvel) $12

Colossal Boy - *Action Comics* #267 aug 1960 (DC) $500

Colossus - *Tales of Suspence* #14 feb 1961 (Marvel) $500

Combat Kelly - *Combat Kelly* #1 nov 1951 (Atlas Comics) $350

Commissioner Gordon - *Detective Comics* #27 may 1939 (DC) $325,000

Conan - *Conan The Barbarian* #1 oct 1970 (Marvel) $450

Crimson Avenger, The - *Detective Comics* #20 oct 1938 (DC) $6,800

Crystal - *Fantastic Four* #45 dec 1965 (Marvel) $195

Cyborg - *DC Comics Presents* #26 oct 1980 (DC) $25

Cyclops - *X-Men* #1 sept 1963 (Marvel) $14,000

Daffy Duck - *Looney Tunes & Merrie Melodies* #1 1941 (Dell) $17,500

Daredevil - *Daredevil* #1 apr 1964 (Marvel) $3,800

Darkhawk - *Darkhawk* #1 mar 1991 (Marvel) $5

Darkseid (cameo) - *Superman's Pal Jimmy Olsen* #134 Dec 1979 (DC) $100

Darkseid (Full App.) - *Forever People* #1 feb 1971 (DC) $75

Darkstars, The - *The Darkstars* #1 oct 1992 (DC) $5

Dazzler - *X-Men* #130 feb 1980 (Marvel) $75

Deadman - *Strange Adventures* #205 oct 1967 (DC) $195

Deathstalker (Full App.) - *Daredevil* #114 jul 1974 (Marvel) $18

Deathstalker (Cameo) - *Daredevil* #113 jun 1974 (Marvel) $18

Defenders - *Marvel Feature* #1 dec 1971 (Marvel) $250

Dennis - *Dennis the Menace* #1 aug 1953 (fawcett) $550

Destroyer Duck - *Destroyer Duck* #1 feb 1982 (Eclipse) $15

Dick Tracy - *Popular Comics* #1 feb 1936 (Dell) $4,600

Doc Octopus - *Amazing Spider-Man* #3 jul 1963 (Marvel) $4,500

Doctor Doom - *Fantastic Four* #5 June 1962 (Marvel) $6,000

Doctor Light – *Justice League of America* #12 jun 1962 (DC) $300

Doctor Solar - *Doctor Solar, Man of the Atom* #1 oct 1962 (Gold Key) $325

Doctor Strange - *Strange Tales* #110 jul 1963 (Marvel) $2,100

Donald Duck - *The Wise Little Hen* #no 1934 (David MaKay\ Whitman) $2,500

Doom Patrol - *My Greatest Adventure* #80 jun 1963 (DC) $725

Dr. Fate - *More Fun Comics* #55 May 1940 (DC) $20,000

Dr. Mid-Nite - *All American Comics* #25 apr 1941 (DC) $12,000

Dracula (Super Hero) - *Dracula* #2 nov 1966 (Dell) $60

E-Man - *E-Man* #1 oct 1973 (Charlton) $30

Electro - *Amazing Spider-Man* #9 feb 1964 (Marvel) $2,000

Elektra - *Daredevil* #168 mar 1981 (marvel) $95

Elementals, The - *Justice Machine, The Annual* #1 - jan 1984 (Noble Comics) $5

Ellery Queen - *Crackerjack Funnies* #23 may 1940 (Dell) $350

Elmer Fudd - *Looney Tunes & Merrie Melodies* 1941 (Dell) $17,500

Elongated Man - *Flash* #112 Apr 1960 (DC) $700

Enforcers - *Amazing Spider-Man* #10 mar 1964 (Marvel) $1,800

Excalibur - *Excalibur* Special Edition no number 1988 (Marvel) $8

Falcon, The - *Pep Comics* #1 jan 1940 (MLJ Mag\Archie) $12,00

Falcon, The (New) - *Captain America* #117 sept 1969 (Marvel) $75

Fantastic Four - *Fantastic Four* #1 nov 1961 (Marvel) $35,000

Femforce - *Femforce* Special #1 Fall 1984 (Americomics) $5

Fiery Mask - *Daring Mystery Comics* #1 Jan 1940 (Timely) $28,000

Firestar - *X-Men* #193 apr 1985 (Marvel) $10

Firestorm - *Firestorm #1* mar 1978 (DC) $10

Flash Thompson - *Amazing Fantasy #15* aug 1962 (Marvel) $58,000

Flash, The (Golden Age) - *Flash Comics #1* jan 1940 (DC) $110,000

Flash, The (Silver Age) - *Showcase #4* sept 1956 (DC) $50,000

Flinstones - *Dell Giant #48* jul 1961 (Dell Pub.) $350

Fly Girl - *#14* with costume sept 1961 (Archie/Radio Comics) $100

Fly Girl - *Adventures of the Fly* w\o costume *#13* jul 1961 (Archie\Radio) $75

Fly, The - *Double Life of Private Stronge, The #1* june 1959 (Archie\Radio) $1,200

Foggy Nelson - *Daredevil #1* apr 1964 (Marvel) $3,800

Forever People - *Forever People #1* feb 1971 (DC) $75

Frightful Four - *Fantastic Four #36* oct 1964 (Marvel) $150

Fu Manchu - *Detective Comics #17* jul 1938 (DC) $4,200

Galactus - *Fantastic Four #48* mar 1966 (Marvel) $1,750

Gambit (Cameo) - *X-Men An. #14* 1990 (Marvel) $40

Gambit (Full App.) - *X-Men #266* Aug 1990 (Marvel) $50

Ghost Rider (Hero) - *Marvel Spotlight #5* aug 1972 (Marvel) $125

Ghost Rider (Western) - *Ghost Rider #1* feb 1967 (Marvel) $75

Giant-Man (Ant-Man) - *Tales to Astonish #49* nov 1963 (Marvel) $275

Gladiator, The - *Daredevil #18* jul 1966 (Marvel) $100

Green Arrow (Golden Age) - *More Fun Comics #73* nov 1941 (DC) $18,000

Green Falcon, The - *Blue Ribbon Comics #4* jun 1940 (MLJ Magazines) $1,000

Green Goblin - *Amazing Spider-Man #14* jul 1964 (Mavel) $3,200

Green Goblin 2 (Harry Osborn) - *Amazing Spider-Man #136* sept 1974 (Marvel) $50

Green Hornet (Golden Age) - *Green Hornet Comics #1* dec 1940 (Helnit/Harvey) $6,000

Green Hornet (Sivler Age) - *Green Hornet #1* feb 1967 (Dell) $300

Green Lantern (Golden Age) - *All-American Comics #16* jul 1940 (DC) $125,000

Green Lantern (Kyle Rayner) - *3rd Series Green Lantern #50* Mar 1994 (DC) $10

Green Lantern (Silver Age) - *Showcase #22* sept 1959 (DC) $7,500

Green Mask, The - *Mystery Men Comics #1* aug 1939 (Fox Features) $15,000

Groo The Wanderer - *Destroyer Duck #1* feb 1982 (Eclipse Comics) $15

Guardians of the Galaxy - *Marvel Super-Heroes #18* jan 1969 (Marvel) $50

Gwen Stacy - *Amazing Spider-Man #31* dec 1965 (Marvel) $350

Harlequin (Joker's Daughter) - *Teen Titans #46* 1977 (DC) $25

Harlequin (Villain - *All-American Comics #89* sept 1947 (DC) $1,400

Harry Osborn - *Amazing Spider-Man #31* dec 1965 (Marvel) $350

Hawk & Dove - *Showcase #75* jul 67 (DC) $175

Hawkeye (Goliath) - *Tales of Suspense #57* sept 1964 (Marvel) $300

Hawkgirl (Shiera Sanders) - *All Star Comics* #5 jun 1941 (DC) $7,200
Hawkman (Golden Age) - *Flash Comics* #1 jan 1940 (DC) $110,000
Hawkman (Silver Age) - *Brave & the Bold* #34 feb 1961 (DC) $3,200
Heckle & Jeckle - *Terry-toons Comics* #50 nov 1946 (Timely\Marvel) $400
Hercules - *Blue Ribbon Comics* #4 jun 1940 MLJ (Magazines) $1,000
Herman & Katnip - *Harvey Comics Hits* #60 sept 1952 (Harvey Pub.) $400
Herman the Mouse - *Casper, The Friendly Ghost* #1 sept 1949 (St. John) $2,100
Hobgoblin 1 - (Ned Leeds) - *Amazing Spider-Man* #238 mar 1983 (Marvel) $75
Hobgoblin 2 (Jack O'Lantern) - *Amazing Spider-Man* #289 jun 1987 (Marvel) $25
Hobgoblin (new) - *Spectacular Spider-Man* #147 mar 1983 (Marvel) $15
Hourman, The - *Adventure Comics* #48 mar 1940 (DC) $34,000
Howard the Duck - *Fear* #19 dec 1973 (Marvel) $25
Hulk, The - *Incredible Hulk* #1 may 1962 (Marvel) $21,000
Human Fly - *Amazing Spider-Man* Annual #10 1976 (Marvel) $25
Human Torch - *Marvel Comics* #1 oct 1939 (Timely) $295,000
Human Torch (Johnny Storm) - *Fantastic Four* #1 nov 1961 (Marvel) $35,000
Iceman - *X-Men* #1 sept 1963 (Marvel) $14,000
Inhumans - *Fantastic Four* #45 dec 1965 (Marvel) $195
Invaders, The - *Avengers* #71 dec 1969 (Marvel) $60

Invisible Girl, The (Sue Storm) - *Fantastic Four* #1 nov 1961 (Marvel) $35,000
Invisible Kid - *Action Comics* #267 aug 1960 (DC) $500
Iron Fist - *Marvel Premiere* #15 may 1974 (Marvel) $100
Iron Man - *Tales of Suspense* #39 mar 1963 (Marvel) $7,000
J. Jonah Jameson - *Amazing Spider-Man* #1 mar 1963 (Marvel) $40,000
Jack of Hearts - *Deadly Hands of Kung Fu* #22 (cameo) (Marvel) $20
Jackal, The - *Amazing Spider-Man* #129 feb 1974 (Marvel) $300
Jaguar, The - *Adventures of the Jaguar* #1 sept 1961 (Archie\Radio) $250
Jason Bard - *Detective Comics* #392 oct 1969 (DC) $40
Jason Todd - *Batman* #357 mar 1983 (DC) $15
Jimmy Olsen - *Action Comics* #1 jun 1938 (DC) $325,000
Joe Robertson - *Amazing Spider-Man* #52 sept 1967 (Marvel) $175
Johnny Quick - *More Fun Comics* #71 sept 1941 (DC) $7,200
Johnny Thunder - *All-American Comics* #100 aug 1948 (DC) $2,500
Johnny Thunder (Hero) - *Flash Comics* #1 jan 1940 (DC) $110,000
Joker, The - *Batman* #1 spring 1940 (DC) $125,000
Jubilee - *X-Men* #244 feb 1989 (Marvel) $40
Juggernaut - *X-Men* #12 jul 1965 (Marvel) $750
Jughead - *Pep Comics* #22 dec 1941 (MLJ Mag.) $21,000
Jughead Jones - *Pep Comics* #22 dec 1941 (MLJ Pub.\Archie) $21,000
Jungle Jim - *Ace Comics* #1 apr 1937 (David McKay) $4,200

Justice League of America - *Brave & the Bold* #28 feb 1960 (DC) $8,500

Justice Society of America - *All Star Comics* #3 win 1940 (DC) $52,000

Kanjar Ro - *Justice League of America* #3 feb 1961 (DC) $975

Karen Page - *Daredevil* #1 apr 1964 (Marvel) $3,800

Kazar(Golden Age) - *Marvel Comics* #1 oct 1939 (Timely) $295,000

Kazar(Silver Age) - *X-Men* #10 (Marvel) $625

Kid Flash - *Flash* #110 dec 1959 (DC) $2,100

Kill Cat - *Deadly Duo, The* #1 nov 1994 (Image) $3

Kingpin, The - *Amazing Spider-Man* #50 jul 1967 (Marvel) $750

Kitty Pride - *X-Men* #129 jan 1980 (Marvel) $95

Kraven the Hunter - *Amazing Spider-Man* #15 aug 1964 (Marvel) $1,200

Krypto - *Adventure Comics* #210 mar 1955 (DC) $4,500

Kull - *Creatures on the Loose* #10 mar 1971 (Marvel) $60

Kull (cameo) - *Conan the Babarian* #1 oct 1970 (Marvel) $450

Lady Death - *Evil Ernie* #1 dec 1991 (Eternity Comics) $75

Legion of Super Heroes - *Adventure Comics* #247 apr 1958 (DC) $7,500

Lex Luthor - *Action Comics* #23 may 1940 (DC) $9,000

Lightning Boy (Lad) - *Adventure Comics* #247 apr 1958 (DC) $7,500

Little Audrey - *Little Audrey* #1 Apr 1948 (ST. John) $425

Little Dot - *Sad Sack Comics* #1 sept 1949 (Harvey) $650

Lizard, The - *Amazing Spider-Man* #6 nov 1963 (Marvel) $2,800

Lois Lane - *Action* #1 jun 1938 (DC) $325,000

Loki - *Journey into Mystery* #85 oct 1962 (Marvel) $1,000

Mad Hatter - *Batman* #49 oct 1948 (DC) $2,000

Mad Hatter - *Detective Comics* #230 apr 1956 (DC) $750

Magneto - *X-Men* #1 sept 1963 (Marvel) $14,000

Magnus - *Robot Fighter* #1 feb 1963 (Gold Key) $350

Martian Manhunter - *Detective Comics* #225 nov 1955 (DC) $8,200

Mary Jane Watson - *Amazing Spider-Man* #25 jun 1965(cameo back view) (Marvel) $525

Mary Jane Watson - *Amazing Spider-Man* #42 nov 1966(face shown) (Marvel) $325

Mary Marvel - *Captain Marvel Adventures* #18 dec 1942 (Fawcett) $2,500

Mask, The - *Exciting Comics* #1 apr 1940 (Nedor\Better Pub.\Standard Comics) $5,200

Master of Kung-Fu (Chang-Chi) - *Special Marvel Edition* #15 dec 1973 (Marvel) $95

Metal Men - *Showcase* #37 mar 1962 (DC) $950

Metamorpho - *Brave & the Bold* #57 dec 1964 (DC) $225

Mickey Mouse - *Four Color* #16 1941 (Dell) $30,000

Mighty Crusaders - *Mighty Crusaders* #1 nov 1965 (Mighty/Radio Comics) $100

Mole Man, The (villain) - *Fantastic Four* #1 nov 1961 (Marvel) $35,000

Molten Man - *Amazing Spider-Man* #28 sept 1965 (Marvel) $725

Moon Knight - *Werewolf By Night* #32 aug 1975 (Marvel) $125

Morbius - *Amazing Spider-Man* #101 oct 1971 (Marvel) $250

Mr. Fantastic (Reed Richards) - *Fantastic Four* #1 nov 1961 (Marvel) $35,000

Mr. Freeze - *Batman* #121 feb 1959 (DC) $525

Mr. Mxyzplik - *Superman* #30 oct 1944 (DC) $3,000

Mr. Terrific - *Sensation Comics* #1 jan 1942 (DC) $42,000

Ms. Marvel - *Ms. Marvel* #1 jan 1977 (Marvel) $15

Mysterio - *Amazing Spider-Man* #13 jun 1964 (Marvel) $1,400

New Gods - *New Gods* #1 feb 1971 (DC) $95

New Mutants - *Marvel Graphic Novel* #4 1982 $15

New Teen Titans - *DC Comics Presents* #26 oct 1980 (DC) $25

New X-Men - *GS X-Men* #1 sum 1975 (Marvel) $1,500

Next Men - *Dark Horse Presents* #54 sept 1991 (Dark Horse) $5

Nick Fury (Shield) - *Strange Tales* #135 aug 1965 (Marvel) $195

Night Force - *New Teen Titans* #21 jul 1982 (DC) $5

Nightcrawler - *GS X-Men* #1 1975 (Marvel) $1,500

Nighthawk - *Avengers* #71 dec 1969 (Marvel) $75

Nyoka, The Jungle Girl - *Jungle Girl* #1 fall 1942 (Fawcett) $1,200

Omega Men - *Green Lantern* #141 jun 1981 (DC) $5

Orion - *New Gods* #1 feb 1971 (DC) $95

Outsiders - *Brave & the Bold* #200 jul 1983 (DC) $12

Owl, The (hero) - *Crackerjack Funnies* #25 jul 1940 (Dell) $1,100

Owl, The (villain) - *Daredevil* #3 aug 1964 (Marvel) $550

Paladin - *Daredevil* #150 feb 1978 (Marvel) $15

Pebbles - *Flinstones* #11 jun 1963 (Gold Key) $100

Penguin, The - *Detective Comics* #58 dec 1941 (DC) $6,000

Perry White - *Superman* #7 nov 1940 (DC) $4,000

Phantom Girl - *Action Comics* #276 may 1961 (DC) $250

Phoenix - *X-Men* #101 oct 1976 (Marvel) $195

Plastic Man - *Police Comics* #1 aug 1941 (Quality Comics) $10,000

Prince Valiant - *Ace Comics* #26 may 1939 (David McKay) $1,200

Professor X - *X-Men* #1 sept 1963 (Marvel) $14,000

Prowler - *Amazing Spider-Man* #78 nov 1969 (Marvel) $110

Puma - *Amazing Spider-Man* #256 sept 1984 (Marvel) $7

Punisher, The - *Amazing Spider-Man* #129 feb 1974 (Marvel) $395

Puppet Master - *Fantastic Four* #8 nov 1962 (Marvel) $1,500

Quicksilver (Golden Age) - *National Comics* #5 nov 1940 (Quality Comics) $1,750

Quicksilver (Silver Age) - *X-Men* #4 mar 1964 (Marvel) $1,400

Raven - *DC Comics Presents* #26 oct 1980 (DC) $25

Raven - *Thunder Agents* #8 sept 1966 (Tower Comics) $60

Red Ryder - *Crackerjack Funnies* #9 mar 1939 (Dell) $1,800

Red Skull - *Captain America Comics* #1 mar 1941 (Marvel) $100,000

Red Sonja - *Conan the Barbarian* #23 feb 1973 (Marvel) $50

Red Tornado - *All-American Comics* #20 nov 1940 (DC) $7,000

Red Wolf - *Avengers* #80 sept 1970 (Marvel) $32

Richie Rich - *Little Dot* #1 Sept 1953 (Harvey) $1,500

Riddler, The - *Detective Comics* #140 oct 1948 (DC) $6,500

Rino, The - *Amazing Spider-Man* #41 oct 1966 (Marvel) $425

Ripley's Believe It or Not - *Ace Comics* #1 apr 1937 (David McKay) $4,200

Robin the Boy Wonder - *Detective Comics* #38 apr 1940 (DC) $50,000

Robocop - *Robocop* #1 oct 1987 (Marvel) $5

Rocketeer (Cameo) - *Starslayer* #1 feb 1982 (PC) $8

Rocketeer (Full App.) - *Starslyer* #2 apr 1982 (PC) $10

Rogue - *Avengers* An. #10 1981 (Marvel) $45

Rom - *Rom* #1 dec 1979 (Marvel) $10

Rose - *Amazing Spider-Man* #253 jun 1984 (Marvel) $7

S.H.I.E.L.D. - *Nick Fury Agent of Shield* #1 jun 1968 (Marvel) $150

Sabertooth - *Iron Fist* #14 aug 1977 (Marvel) $150

Sabrina the Teen-age Witch - *Archie's Madhouse* #22 oct 1962 (Archie) $300

Sad Sack - *True Comics* #55 dec 1946 (True Comics\Parents Mag.) $75

Samson - *Fantastic Comics* #1 dec 1939 (Fox Features) $6,200

Sandman, The (hero) - *New York World's Fair* 1939 (DC) $32,000

Sandman, The (villian) - *Amazing Spider-Man* #4 sept 1963 (Marvel) $3,500

Sasquatch - *X-Men* #120 apr 1979 (Marvel) $110

Sauron - *X-Men* #60 (Marvel) $150

Scarlet Witch - *X-Men* #4 mar 1964 (Marvel) $1,400

Schemer (Richard Fisk) - *Amazing Spider-Man* #83 apr 1970 (Marvel) $125

Scorpion, The - *Amazing Spider-Man* #20 jan 1965 (Marvel) $900

Sea Devils - *Showcase* #27 jul 1960 (DC) $1,200

Sgt. Bilko - *Sgt Bilko* #1 may 1957 (DC) $750

Sgt. Fury - *Sgt. Fury* #1 may 1963 (Marvel) $2,000

Sgt. Rock - *Our Army at War* #81 apr 1959 (DC) $3,000

Shadow - *Shadow Comics* #1 mar 1940 (Street & Smith) $5,000

Shadow, The - *The Shadow* #1 oct 1973 (DC) $30

Shazam (Capt. Marvel) - *Shazam* #1 feb 1973 (DC) $30

She Hulk - *Savage She Hulk* #1 feb 1980 (Marvel) $15

Sheena - *Jumbo Comics* #1 Sept 1938 (Fiction House) $20,000

Shield - *Pep Comics* #1 jan 1940 (MLJ Mags) $12,500

Shocker, The - *Amazing Spider-Man* #46 mar 1967 (Marvel) $275

Shrinking Violet - *Action Comics* #276 may 1961 (DC) $250

Silver Sable - *Amazing Spider-Man* #265 jun 1985 (Marvel) $15

Silver Surfer - *Fantastic Four* #48 mar 1966 (Marvel) $1,750

Sinestro - *Green Lantern* #7 jul 1961 (DC) $375

Snapper Carr - *Brave & the Bold* #28 feb 1960 (DC) $8,500

Solomon Grundy - *All-American Comics* #61 nov 1944 (DC) $7,500

Son of Satan (Cameo) - *Ghost Rider* #1 sept 1973 (Marvel) $95

Son of Satan (Full App.) - *Ghost Rider* #2 (Marvel) $25

Space Ranger - *Showcase* #15 jul 1958 (DC) $2,500

Spawn - *Spawn* #1 may 1992 (Image Comics) $30

Spectre - *More Fun Comics* #52 feb 1940 (DC) $75,000

Spectre (1st Full Costume) - *More Fun Comics* #54 apr 1940 (DC) $15,000

Speed Racer - *Dai Kamikaze* #1 jun 1987 (Now) $3

Speedy - *More Fun Comics* #73 nov 1941 (DC) $18,000

Spider Woman - *Marvel Spotlight* #32 feb 1977 (Marvel) $25

Spider-Man - *Amazing Fantasy* #15 aug 1962 (Marvel) $58,000

Spirit - *Police Comics* #11 sept 1942 (Quality Comics) $2,500

Spy Smasher - *Whiz Comics* #1 feb 1940 (Fawcett) $125,000

Starhawk - *Defenders, The* #27 (cameo) sept 1975 (Marvel) $10

Starhawk - *Defenders, The* #28 (full app.) oct 1976 (Marvel) $10

Starman - *Adventure Comics* #61 apr 1941 (DC) $18,000

Starslayer - *Starslyer* #1 feb 1982 (PC) $8

Storm - *GS X-Men* #1 1975 (Marvel) $1,500

Sub-Mariner (Golden Age) - *Marvel Comics* #1 oct 1939 (Timely) $295,000

Sub-Mariner (Silver Age) - *Fantastic Four* #4 may 1962 (Marvel) $5,200

Suicide Squad - *Brave & the Bold* #25 aug 1959 (DC) $625

Sun Boy - *Action Comics* #276 may 1961 (DC) $250

Sunfire - *X-Men* #64 jan 1970 (Marvel) $150

Super Rabbit - *Comedy Comics* #14 mar 1943 (Timely) $600

Superboy - *More Fun Comics* #101 jan 1945 (DC) $11,500

Superfriends - *Superfreinds* #1 nov 1976 (DC) $45

Supergirl - *Action Comics* #252 may 1959 (DC) $2,750

Superman - *Action Comics* #1 jun 1938 (DC) $325,000

Swamp Thing - *House of Secrets* #92 jun 1971 (DC) $750

Swordsman, The - *Avengers* #19 aug 1965 (Marvel) $150

Tarantula - *Amazing Spider-Man* #134 jul 1974 (Marvel) $65

Tarzan - *Tip Top Comics* #1 apr 1936 (United Features) $9,000

Teen Titans - *Brave & the Bold* #54 jun 1964 (DC) $400

Teenage Mutant Ninja Turtles - *Teenage Mutant Ninja Turtles* #1 1984 (Mirage Studios) $300

Thing, The (Ben Grimm) - *Fantastic Four* #1 nov 1961 (Marvel) $35,000

Thor (Beta Ray Bill) - *Thor* #337 nov 1983 (Marvel) $10

Thor (Dargo) - *Thor* #384 oct 1987 (Marvel) $7

Thor (Don Blake) - *Journey into Mystery* #83 aug 1962 (Marvel) $7,200

Thor (Eric Masterson) - *Thor* #433 jun 1991 (Marvel) $5

Thunder Agents - *Thunder Agents* #1 nov 1965 (JC Comics/Archie) $250

Thunderbird - *GS X-Men* #1 1975 (Marvel) $1,500

Tick, The- *Tick, The* #1 jun 1988 (New England Comics) $50

Tom & Jerry - *Our Gang Comics* #1 sept 1942 (Dell) $1,250

Tom Mix - *Comics, The* #1 mar 1937 (Dell) $2,800

Tomahawk - *Star Spangled Comics* #69 jun 1947 (DC) $1,250

Tommy Tomorrow - *Real Fact Comics* #6 jan 1947 (DC) $1,400

Torchy - *Doll Man Quarterly, The* #8 spring 1946 (Quality Comics) $2,000

Toro - *Human Torch* #2(1) Fall 1940 (Timely\Marvel) $38,000

Transformers - *Transformers* #1 sept 1984 (Marvel) $18

Triplicate Girl - *Action Comics* #276 may 1961 (DC) $250

Turok - *Four Color* #596 dec 1954 (Dell) $850

Two Face - *Detective Comics* #66 aug 1942 ((DC) $5,000

Typhoid Mary - *Daredevil* #254 may 1988 (Marvel) $10

Uncle Ben - *Amazing Fantasy* #15 aug 1962 (Marvel) $58,000

Uncle Scrooge - *Four Color* #178 dec 1947 (Dell) $1,500

Underdog - *Underdog* #1 jul 1970 (Charlton Comics) $85

Usagi Yojimbo - *Albedo* #2 apr 1985 (Thoughts & Images) $15

Vampirella - *Vampirella* #1 sept 1969 (Warren Pub.) $650

Venom (Cameo) - *Amazing Spider-Man* #298 mar 1988 (Marvel) $40

Venom (full with costume) -*Amazing Spider-Man* #300 may 1988 (Marvel) $95

Veronica Lodge - *Pep Comics* #26 apr 1942 (MLJ Mag.) $1,950

Viking Prince - *Brave & the Bold* #1 aug 1955 (DC) $5,200

Vision (Golden Age) - *Marvel Mystery Comics* #13 nov 1940 (Timely\Marvel) $6,200

Vision (Silver Age) - *Avengers* #57 oct 1968 (Marvel) $125

Vulture, The - *Amazing Spider-Man* #2 may 1963 (Marvel) $6,200

Warlord - *First Issue Special* #8 (DC) $25

Wasp - *Tales To Astonish* #44 jun 1963 (Marvel) $525

Watcher, The - *Fantastic Four* #13 apr 1963 (Marvel) $750

Wendigo - *Incredible Hulk* #162 apr 1973 (Marvel) $30

Werewolf by Night - *Marvel Spotlight* #2 jan 1972 (Marvel)

Wildcat - *Sensation Comics* #1 jan 1942 (DC) $42,000

Witchblade - *Cyblade\Shi* #1 1995 (Image) $50

Wolverine (Cameo) - *Incredible Hulk* #180 (Marvel) $150

Wolverine (Full App) - *Incredible Hulk* #181 (Marvel) $1,200

Wonder Girl - *Wonder Woman* #107 jul 1961 (DC) $275

Wonder Girl (Donna Troy) *Brave & the Bold* #60 jun 1965 (DC) $125

Wonder Man - *Startling Comics* #1 jun 1940 (Better Pub.) $3,000

Wonder Woman - *All Star* #8 dec 1941 (DC) $45,000

Woody Woodpecker - *Funnies, The* #64 may 1942 (Dell) $1,200

X-Factor - *Avengers* #263 jan 1986 (Marvel) $10

X-Men - *X-Men* #1 sept 1963 (Marvel) $14,000

Yogi Bear - *Four Color* #1067 dec 1959 (Dell) $150

Yosemite Sam - *Yosemite Sam* #1 dec 1970 (Gold Key) $50

Young Allies - *Young Allies* #1 sum 1941 (Timely) $18,000

Young Justice - *Young Justice: The Secret* jun 1998 (DC) $5

Zatanna - *Hawkman* #4 oct 1964
(DC) $250
Zorro - *Four Color* #228 may 1949
(Dell) $295

FOCUS OF THIS ISSUE IS ON - SPIDER-MAN

The following is a comprehensive list of Spider-Man appearances including cameo's and key appearances of other related characters.

Amazing Fantasy

#15 aug\62 F & O - Spider-Man, 1st - Aunt May, Uncle Ben, Flash Thompson, and The Burglar
                        $58,000
#16 dec\96, #17 jan\96, #18 mar\96
                        $4

Amazing Spider-Man

#1 mar\63 1st - J. Jonah Jameson, John Jameson, Chameleon $40,000
#2 may\63 1st - Vulture and Terrible Tinkerer $6,200
#3 jul\63 1st - Doc Octopus $4,500
#4 Sept\63 1st & O - Sandman, 1st - Betty Brant $3,500
#5 oct\63 Dr. Doom and The Fantastic Four $2,600
#6 nov\63 1st - Lizard and Dr. Connors $2,800
#7 dec\63 vulture $1,600
#8 jan\64 Human Torch, 1st - Living Brain $1,600
#9 feb\64 1st & O – Electro $2,000
#10 mar\64 1st – Enforcers $1,800
#11 and #12 apr and may\64 Both Doc Octopus $1,200
#13 jun\64 1st – Mysterio $1,400
#14 jul\64 Enforcers, 1st - Green Goblin $3,200
#15 aug\64 Chameleon, 1st - Kraven the Hunter $1,200
#16 sept\64 Daredevil and Ringmaster $800
#17 oct\64 Human Torch, 2nd Green Goblin $1,200

#18 nov\64 Sandman 1st - Ned Leeds and Anna Watson $775
#19 dec\64 Human Torch, Sandman, Enforcers $625
#20 jan\65 1st & O – Scorpion $900
#21 feb\65 Human Torch, The Beetle $625
#22 mar\65 Ringmaster, 1st - Princess Python $575
#23 apr\65 3rd Green Goblin $800
#24 may\65 Dr. Rinehart (Mysterio) $475
#25 jun\65 1st - Spencer Smythe and Spider-Slayer 1st - Mary Jane Watson (no face shown) $525
#26 jul\65 Green Goblin, 1st - Crime Master $595
#27 aug\65 Green Goblin, Crime Master $595
#28 sept\65 Spider-Slayer 1st & O - Molten Man $725
#29 oct\65 Scorpion $375
#30 nov\65 1st - Cat Burglar $375
#31 dec\65 Doc Octopus, 1st - Gwen Stacy and Harry Osborn
                        $350
#32 jan\66 Doc Octopus, #33 feb\66 Master Planner's Henchmen #34 mar\66 Kraven, #35 apr\66 Molten Man, #36 may\66 1st – Looter
                        $295
#37 jun\66 1st - Mendel Stromm (Robot Master) and Norman Osborn #38 jul\66 2nd Mary Jane Watson (no face shown) $325
#39 aug\66 Green Goblin $475
#40 Sept\66 O - Green Goblin $625
#41 oct\66 1st – Rino $425
#42 nov\66 Rino, 1st - Mary Jane Watsonface shown) $325
#43 dec\66 Rino, #44 jan\67 Lizard, #45 feb\67 Lizard $250
#46 mar\67 1st – Shocker $275
#47 apr\67 Kraven $250
#48 may\67 1st - Vulture II (Blackie Drago) $275
#49 Jun\67 Vulture II, Kraven $250

#50 Jul\67 1st – Kingpin $750
#51 aug\67 2nd Kingpin $375
#52 sept\67 Kingpin 1st - Joe
  Robertson $175
#53 oct\67 Doc Octopus, #54
  nov\67 Doc Octopus, #55 dec\67
  Doc Octopus, #56 jan\68 Doc
  Octopus 1st - Capt. G. Stacy $175
#57 feb\68 Kazar and Zabu, #58
  mar\68 Kazar, Zabu and Spider-
  Slayer, #59 apr\68 Brainwasher
  (Kingpin), #60 may\68 Brainwasher (Kingpin) $160
#61 jun\68 Kingpin, #62 jul\68
  Medusa, #63 aug\68 Vultire II, #64
  sept\68 Vulture, #65 oct\68 Prison
  Inmates, #66 nov\68 Mysterio, #67
  dec\68 Mysterio, #68 jan\69
  Kingpin, #69 feb\69 Kingpin, #70
  mar\69 Kingpin, #71 apr\69
  Quicksilver and The Scarlet Witch,
  #72 may\69 Shocker $125
#73 jun\69 1st – Silvermane $150
#74 jul\69 Silvermane (last 12¢
  issue) $150
#75 aug\69 Silvermane (first 15¢
  issue), #76 SEPT\69 Human Torch,
  Lizard #77 oct\69 Human Torch,
  Lizard, #79 dec\69 Prowler, #80
  jan\70 Chameleon, #82 mar\70
  Electro, #84 may\70 Schemer,
  Kingpin, #85 jun\70 Schemer,
  Kingpin, #86 july\70 O - Black
  Widow , #87 aug\70 Prowler, #88
  sept\70 Doc Octopus #89 oct\70
  Doc Octopus, #91 dec\70 F- Sam
  Bullit, #92 jan\71 Iceman, Sam
  Bullit #93 feb\71 Prowler #95
  apr\71 Terrorists $95
#78 nov\69 1st - Prowler, #81 feb\70
  1st – Kangaroo $110
#83 apr\70 1st – Schemer (Richard
  Fisk), Kingpin $125
#90 nov\70 Death Of Capt. G. Stacy,
  Doc Octopus $150
#94 mar\71 Beetle O - Spider-Man
  Retold $150

#96 may\71, #97 jun\71, #98 jul\71
  Green Goblin in all (not approved
  by CCA) Drug Stories $195
#99 aug\71 1st – Turpo (prisoner)
                                        $95
#100 sept\71 app. by Vulture, Doc
  Octopus, Lizard, Green Goblin,
  Kingpin 1st - six armed Spider-
  Man $395
#101 oct\71 Lizard 1st - Morbius
  (last 15¢ issue) $250
#102 nov\71 Lizard, Morbius (25¢
  issue) $175
#103 dec\71 Kazar, Zabu, Kraven 1st
  – Gog (first 20¢ issue), #104
  jan\72 Kazar, Zabu, Kraven, Gog,
  #105 feb\72 Spider-Slayer III, #106
  mar\72 Spider-Slayer III, #107
  apr\72 Spider-Slayer III, #109
  jun\72 Dr. Strange, The Giant One,
  #111 aug\72 Gibbon, Kraven #112
  sept\72 Gibbon, Doc Octopus,
  #114 nov\72 Dr. Octopus,
  Hammerhead, #115 dec\72 Dr.
  Octopus, Hammerhead, #116
  jan\73 The Smasher, #117 feb\73
  The Smasher, 1st - Disruptor,
  #118 mar\73 Disruptor, Smasher
                                        $65
#108 may\72 1st - Sha-Shan and The
  Giant One, #110 jul\72 1st -
  Gibbon, Kraven, #113 oct\72 Doc
  Octopus, 1st – Hammerhead $75
#119 apr\73, #120 may\73 Hulk in
  both $100
#121 jun\73 Death of Gwen Stacy,
  Green Goblin $275
#122 Jul\73 Death of the Green
  Goblin $325
#123 aug\73 Luke Cage, #126
  nov\73 Death Kangaroo, #128
  jan\74 Vulture III #130 mar\74
  Human Torch, Hammerhead,
  Jackel, Doc Octopus $50
#124 sept\73 1st - Man Wolf $75
#125 oct\73 O - Man Wolf $60
#127 dec\73 1st - Vulture III $60

#129 feb\74 1st - Punisher and Jackel $395

#131 apr\74 Doc octopus, Hammerhead (last 20¢ issue), #132 may\74 molten (first 25¢ issue) #133 jun\74 Molten Man $40

#134 jul\74 1st – Tarantula $65

#135 aug\74 Tarantula, 2nd Punisher $95

#136 sept\74 1st - Green Goblin II (Harry Osborn) $95

#137 oct\74 Green Goblin II $70

#138 nov\74 1st - Mindworm, #139 dec\74 Jackel, 1st - Grizzly, #140 jan\75 Grizzly, Jackel, #141 feb\75 1st - Mysterio II, #142 mar\75 Mysterio II $28

#143 apr\75 1st – Syclone $40

#144 may\75 Syclone, Gwen Stacy Clone #145 jun\75 Scorpion,#146 jul\75 Scorpion, Jackel, #147 aug\75 Tarantula, Jackel $30

#148 sept\75 Tatrantula, Jackel revealed $35

#149 oct\75 1st - Spider-Man Clone, Jackel, Tarantula $75

#150 nov\75 Vulture, Kingpin, Sandman, Spider-Slayer #151 dec\75 Shocker, (Spider-Man Clone in both) $32

#152 jan\76 Shocker, #153 feb\76 The Deadliest Hundred Yards, #154 mar\76 Sandman, #157 jun\76 Doc Octopus, Hammerhead, #158 jul\76 Doc Octopus, Hammerhead #160 Sept\76 Terrible Tinkerer, Toy (first 30¢ issue) $25

#155 apr\76 1st - Tallon, #156 may\76 Doc Octopus 1st - Mirage, #159 aug\76 1st – Toy (last 25¢ issue) $28

#155 – #159 (30¢ covers 50% more) #161 oct\76 Nightcrawler, Wolveine, Colossus, Punisher $32

#162 nov\76 Nightcrawler, Punisher 1st – Jigsaw $30

#163 dec\76 Kingpin #164 jan\77 Kingpin #165 feb\77 Stegron, Lizard, #166 mar\77 Stegron, Lizard, Spider-Slayer IV #168 may\77 Spider-Slayer IV, Will-O'-The-Wisp #169 jun\77 Dr. Faustus, #170 jul\77 Dr. Faustus, Burglar, #171 aug\77 Photon, Nova #173 oct\77 Hitman, Punisher (last 30¢ issue) $16

#167 apr\77 Spider-Slayer IV, 1st - Will-O'-The-Wisp, #172 sept\77 Molten Man, 1st - Rocket Racer, #174 nov\77 Punisher, Hitman #175 dec\77 Punisher, Hitman $18

#169 – 173 (35¢ covers 25% more)

#176 jan\78 1st - Green Goblin III $22

#177 feb\78 #178 mar\78 #179 apr\78 Green Goblin III, Silvermane in all $20

#180 may\78 Death of Goblin III, Goblin II, Silvermane $22

#181 jun\78 O - Spider-Man (cameo galore) $15

#182 jul\78 Rocket Racer, 1st - Jackson Wheele, #183 aug\78 Terreble Tinkerer, Toy, Rocket Racer, 1st - (Death) Big Wheele, #184 sept\78 1st - White Dragon $14

#185 oct\78 White Dragon, #186 nov\78 Chameleon, #187 dec\78 Capt. America, Electro, #188 jan\79 Jigsaw, #189 feb\79 Man wolf, Spenser Smythe, #190 mar\79 Man wolf, Spenser Smythe $12

#191 apr\79 Spencer Smythe 1st - Spider-Slayer V (last 35¢ issue), #192 may\79 Death of Spencer Smythe, Human Fly (first 40¢ issue), #193 jun\79 Human Fly, Dr. Rinehart (Myserio), Burglar, #196 sept\79 Dr. Rinehart (Mysterio), Kingpin, #197 oct\79 Dr. Rinehart (Myserio), Burglar Kingpin, #198

nov\79 Myserio, Burglar #199 dec\79 Burglar, Mysterio $10
#194 jul\79 Dr Rinehart (Mysterio), Burglar, 1st - Black Cat $25
#195 aug\79 Dr Rinehart (Mysterio), Burglar, O - Black Cat $15
#200 jan\80 (75¢ cover) Death of the Burgalar $30
#201 feb\80 Punisher, #202 mar\80 Punisher $10
#203 apr\80 Dazzler, Light Master, #204 may\80 Black Cat, #205 jun\80 Black Cat, #206 jul\80 Jonas Harrow #207 aug\80 Mesmero, #211 dec\80 Sub-Mariner, #213 feb\81 Wizard, Llyra, #216 may\81 Madam Web #217 jun\81 Hydro-Man, Sandman #218 jul\81 Daredevil, Hydro-Man, Sandman, #219 aug\81 Daredevil, Grey Gargoyle, Jonas Harrow, #220 sept\81 Moon Knight, Monsters $8
#208 Sept\80 1st - Fusion, #209 oct\80 1st - Calypso, Kraven, #210 nov\80 1st - Madam Web #212 jan\81 1st - Hydro-Man $12
#214 mar\81 Sub-Mariner, Frightful Four(Wizard, Llyra, Sandman, Trapster),#215 apr\81 Sub-Mariner, Mr. Fantastic, Invisible Girl, Thing, Frightful Four $10
#221 oct\81 Ramrod, #223 dec\81 Red Ghost, Super-Apes (last 50¢ issue), #224 jan\82 Vulture (first 60¢ issue) #225 feb\82 Foolkiller, #226 mar\82 Black Cat, #227 apr\82 Black Cat, #228 may\82 Murder By Spider, #229 jun\82 Juggernaut, #230 jul\82 Juggernaut #231 aug\82 Cobra, Mr. Hyde, #232 sept\82 Cobra, Mr. Hyde #233 oct\82 Tarantula, #234 nov\82 Tarantula (F - mutated), Will-O'-The -Wisp, #235 dec\82 Tarantula (mutated), Will-O'-The-Wisp, #237 feb\83 Stilt-Man, #240

may\83 Vulture, #241 jun\83 O – Vulture $7
#222 nov\81 1st - Speed Demon, #236 jan\83 Death Tarantula (mutated), Will-O'-The-Wisp $8
#238 feb\83 1st – Hobgoblin $75
#239 mar\83 2nd Hobgoblin, Madam Web $30
#242 jul\83 Mad Thinker, Awesome Android, #243 aug\83 Black Cat, #246 nov\83 Black Cat, Watcher #247 dec\83 Frog-Man, Thunderball, #248 jan\84 Thunderball, #254 jul\84 Jock O'Lantern, #257 oct\84 Black Cat, Puma, Rose, Kingpin, Arranger $6
#244 sept\83 3rd Hobgoblin, Black Cat $15
#245 oct\83 Hobgoblin, Black Cat $12
#249 feb\84 Kingpin, Hobgoblin, #250 mar\84 Hobgoblin, #251 Apr\84 Hobgoblin $10
#252 may\84 1st - Black Costume, Black Cat, Avengers $40
#253 jun\84 1st - Rose, #255 aug\84 Red Ghost, Super-Apes, 1st - Black Fox, #256 sept\84 Rose, 1st – Puma $7
#258 nov\84 Black Cat, Human Torch, Mr. Fantastic, Puma, Rose, Hobgoblin, #259 Dec\84 She Hulk, Mr. Fantastic, Hobgoblin, Rose, #260 jan\85 Invisible Woman, Franklin Richards, Hobgoblin, Rose #261 feb\85 Rose Hobgoblin $10
#262 mar\85 (photo cover) (last 60¢ issue), #263 apr\85 Black Cat, 1st - Spectacular Spider Kid (first 65¢ issue), #266 jun\85 1st - Misfits (Leap-Frog, Spider-Kid, Toad, Black Cat, #267 aug\85 Human Torch, #268 sept\85 Kingpin, Arranger, #269 oct\85 Firelord, #270 nov\85 Avengers, Firelord, #272 jan\86 Slyde, Puma (last 65¢ issue), #273

feb\86 Puma, Beyonder , #274 mar\86 Puma, Kingpin, Mephisto, Beyonder (first 75¢ issue), #277 jun\86 Hobgoblin, Kingpin, #278 jul\86 Hobgoblin, Death of Wraith, Rose, #279 aug\86 Silver Sable, Jack O'Lantern, #280 sept\86 Silver Sable, Sandman, 1st - Sinister Syndicate(Rhino, Beetle, Speed Demon, Hydro-Man, Boomerang), Kingpin, Rose, Jack O'Lantern, Hobgoblin, #281 oct\86 Sinister Syndicate, Rose, Jack O'Lantern, Hobgoblin, #282 nov\86 X-Factor, #283 dec\86 Wasp, Absorbing Man, Titania, Hobgoblin, #284 jan\87 Hobgoblin, Hammerhead, Rose, Jack O'Lantern, Silvermane, Arranger, #285 feb\87 Punisher, Hobgoblin, Rose, Arranger, Jack O'Lantern, Hammerhead, #286 mar\87 Rose, Hobgoblin, Jack O'Lantern, #287 apr\87 Daredevil, Falcon, Hobgoblin, Kingpin, Rose, Arranger, #288 may\87 Daredevil, Falcon, Black Cat, Hobgoblin, Punisher, Rose, Kingpin, Hammerhead, Jack O'Lantern, #290 jul\87 Mary Jane (The Big Question), #291 aug\87 Alistair Smythe, Spider-Slayer, #292 sept\87 Alistair Smythe, Spider-Slayer, #293 oct\87 Kraven, Vermin, #296 Jan\88 Dr. Octopus, #297 feb\88 Dr. Octopus $6
#264 may\85 1st - Red 9, #271 Dec\85 1st - Manslaughter, #276 may\86 Hobgoblin, Rose, Death of the Fly, Scourge, #294 nov\87 Death of Kraven, Vermin, #295 dec\87 1st - Brain Storm $7
#275 apr\86 ($1.25 cover) Hobgoblin, Rose, Kingpin, Arranger, O - Spider-Man $15
#289 jun\87 ($1.25 cover) Black Cat, Rose, Kingpin, 1st - Hobgoblin II $25

Todd McFarlane Issues #298 - #325, #324 Cover Only
#298 mar\88 Chance 1st - Venom (shadow app.) $42
#299 apr\88 Chance, Venom (Cameo) (last 75¢ issue) $25
#300 may\88 Chance Venom (full), The Thing ($1.50 cover) $95
#301 jun\88 Silver Sable (first $1 cover), #302 jul\88 Silver Sable, Sandman, #303 aug\88 Silver Sable, Sandman, #304 sept\88 Prowler, Black Fox, #305 sept 88 Prowler, Black Fox, #306 oct\88 Black Cat, Humbug, #307 oct\88 Chameleon, #308 nov\88 Task Master, #309 nov\88 1st - Styx & Stone, #310 dec\88 Killer Shrike, #311 jan\89 Mysterio, #313 mar\89 Lizard, #314 apr\89 Down & Out In Forest Hills $15
#312 feb\89 Green Goblin II, Hobgoblin $20
#315 may\89 Venom, Hydro-Man, #316 jun\89 Black Cat Venom, #317 jul\89 The Thing, Venom $18
#318 aug\89 Scorpion, Justin Hammer, #319 Sept\89 Scorpion, Justin Hammer, Rhino, Black Lash, #320 Sept\89 Paladin, Silver Sable, #321 oct\89 Paladin, Silver Sable, #322 Oct\89 Silver Sable, Ultimatum, #323 nov\89 Silver Sable, Capt. America, Paladin, Ultimatum #325 nov\89 Silver Sable, Capt. America, Ultimatum, Red Scull $12
#324 nov\89 Silver Sable Capt. America, Saber Tooth, #328 jan\90 Hulk $10
#326 dec\89 Graviton, #327 dec\89 Magneto, #329 feb\90 Capt. Universe, Loki, Sebastian Shaw, #330 mar\90 Punisher, Black Cat #331 apr\90 Punisher, Venom #332 may\90 Venom, #333 jun\90 Venom $5

#334 jul\90 Iron Man Sinister Six (Doc Octopus, Sandman, Mysterio, Electro, Hobgoblin, Vulture), #335 jul\90 Sinister Six, Shocker, #336 aug\90 Sinister Six, #337 aug\90 Sinister Six, #338 sept\90 Sinister Six, #339 sept\90 Sinister Six, #340 oct\90 Femme Fatales, #341 nov\90 Black Cat, Tarantula, #342 dec\90 Black Cat, Scorpion, #343 jan\91 Black Cat, Tarantula, #348 jun\91 Avengers, #349 jul\91 Black Fox, #351 sept\91 Nova, Tri Sentinals #352 oct\91 nova, Tri Sentinals, #353 nov\91 Darkhawk, Punisher, #354 nov\91 Punisher, Nova, Night Thrasher, Moon Night, #355 dec\91 Punisher, Nova, Night Thrasher, Moon Night, #356 dec\91 Punisher, Nova, Night Thrasher, Moon Night, #357 jan\92 Punisher, Nova, Darkhawk, Moon Night, #358 jan\92 Secret Empire, Punisher, Nova, Night Thrasher, Moon Night, Darkhawk, (last $1 issue),#359 feb\92 Cardiac, Cletus Casady (first $1.25 issue) $3.50

#344 Feb\91 1st Cardiac and Cletus Casady, Rhino $12

#345 mar\91 Cardiac, Cletus Casady, Boomerang, #346 apr\91 Venom, #347 may\91 Venom $7

#350 aug\91 Dr. Doom ($1.50 cover), #360 mar\92 1st – Carnage (cameo),#362 may\92 Carnage, Venom, #363 jun\92 Carnage, Venom $5

#361 apr\92 1st – Carnage (full) $12

#364 jul\92 Shocker, #365 aug\90 1st- Spider-Man 2099, Lizard, #366 sept\92 Capt. America, Red Skull, #367 oct\92 Solo, Red Skull #368 nov\92 Spider-Slayers, #369 nov\92 Electro, Green Goblin, #370 dec\92 Black Cat, Scorpion,

#371 Dec\92 Black Cat, Spider-Slayers, #372 jan\93 Black Cat, Scorpion, #373 jan\93 Spider-Slayers, Venom, #374 feb\93 Venom, #376 apr\93 Cardiac, Styx & Stones, #377 may\93 Cardiac, Styx & Stones, #378 jun\93 Venom, #379 jul\93 Carnage, Venom, #380 aug\93 Carnage, Venom, Capt. America, #381 sept\93 Hulk #382-387, (387 last $1.25 issue), #389 (first $1.50 issue), #390–393, #395–399, #401–407, #409–424, #426–440 $3

#388 ($2.25 cover) $3.50

#388, #394, #397 ($2.95 cover), #425 ($2.99 cover) $4.25

#400 ($3.95 cover bagged), #441 (Final Issue) $5

Amazing Spider-Man

V2 #1 jan 1999 - present

Amazing Spider-Man Annuals

#1 1964 Sinister Six $1,350
#2 - 1965 Dr. Strange $425
#3 - 1966 Avengers, Hulk, Daredevil
                    $195
#4 - 1967 Human Torch, Mysterio
                    $150
#5 - 1968 Fantastic Four $100
#6 - 1969 Sinister Six, #7 - 1970 Chameleon, #8 1971 – Shocker
                    $60
#9 - 1973 Green Goblin $35
#10 - 1976 O - The Fly $25
#11 (1977) – #15 (1980) $15
#16 (1982) – #20 (1986 $8
#21 1987 Wedding (Peter Parker and Mary Jane) $12
#22 (1988) – #28 (1994) $6

Spider- Man Special 1996 – 2001
                    $4

Giant Size Spider-Man (1996 – 2001)

#1 july 1974 Human Torch, Dracula
                    $75
#2 oct 1974 Chang-Chi, #3 jan 1975 Doc Savage $35

#4 apr 1975, 3rd Punisher app. $100
#5 jul 1975 and #6 1975 $20

Amazing Spider-Man Skating On Thin Ice $10

Amazing Spider-Man 1980 Free With Aim $15

Alpha Flight
#1 aug 1983 $6
#74 sept 1989, #75 oct 1989, #121 jun 1993 $3

Avengers
#3 jan 1964 $595
#11 dec 1964 $325
#59 dec 1968, #60 jan 1969 (cameo) $35
#85 feb 1971 (cameo) $28
#100 jun 1972 (cameo) $100
#118 dec 1973 (cameo) $20
#168 feb 1978(cameo) $5
#221 jul 1982, #235 sept 1983 (cameo), #236 oct 1983, #237 nov 1983, #258 aug 1985, #314 feb 1990, #315 mar 1990, #316 apr 1990, #317 may 1990, #318 jun 1990, #329 feb 1991, #330 mar 1991 (cameo),#332 may 1991 (cameo), #333 jun 1991, #400 jul 1996 (cameo), #1.5 dec 1999 $4
Avengers Annual #5 jan 1972 $25

Avengers V3
#1 feb 1998 $6
#10 nov 1998(cameo),#11 dec 1998 (cameo) $3
#25 feb 2000, #51 apr 2002 (cameo) $2.50

Avengers West Coast
#84 jul 1992, #85 aug 1992, #86 sept 1992 $3

Captain America
#137 may 1971, #138 jun 1971 $25
#250 oct 1980 (cameo) $7
#265 jan 1982, #266 feb 1982 $3

Clandestine
#6 mar 1995
#7 apr 1995 $3

Cloak & Dagger
V2 #3 nov 1985 $3

V3 #16 feb 1991, #17 apr 1991, #18 jun 1991 $2

Code of Honor
#1 jan 1997, #2 mar 1997, #4 may 1997 (cameo) $6

Conspiracy
#1 feb 1998 (cameo), #2 mar 1998 (cameo) $3

Contest of Champions
#1 jun 1982, #2 jul 1982(cameo) $8 (Marvel Super Hero)

Contest of Chanpions II
#1 sept 1999 (cameo)
#4 nov 1999, #5 nov 1999(cameo) $3

Cosmic Powers Unlimited
#1 may 1995 (cameo) $2.50

Damage Control
#1 may 1989, V3 #1 jun 1991 $2

Daredevil
#1 aug 1964 $3,800
#16 may 1966, #17 jun 1966 $150
#27 apr 1967 $75
#54 jul 1969 (cameo) $28
#77 jun 1971 $30
#103 sept 1973 $15
#270 sept 1989, #306 jul 1992, #326 mar 1994 (cameo) #354 jul 1996 $3

Volume 2
#8 jun 1999 $4
#16 may 2001, #20 sept 2001, #21 oct 2001 (cameo), #25 dec 2001 (1 page) $3
#35 sept 2002 $2.75
Daredevil Annuals #3 1972 $25
#4(5) 1989 $4

Darkhawk
#2 apr 1991, #3 may 1991, #19 sept 1992, #20 oct 1992 $3

Dazzler
#1 mar 1981, #2 apr 1981, 21 nov 1982 $6

Deadpool
#11 dec 1997

Defenders
#61 jul 1978 $4

#107 may 1982, #108 jun 1982, #109
jul 1982 $3

Defenders
V2 #9 nov 2001 (cameo), #10 dec
2001 (cameo) $2.50

Defenders: The Order
#5 Aug 2002, #6 sept 2002 $2.50

Doctor Strange
#179 apr 1969 $50
V2 #2 aug 1974 $30

Doctor Strange, Sorcerer Supreme
#10 nov 1989 (cameo), #14 feb 1990
(cameo)#32 aug 1991(cameo),
#33 sept 1991 (cameo),#55 jul
1993 (cameo), #61 jan 1994
(cameo) $3

Excalibur
#53 aug 1992, #125 oct 1998
(cameo) $3

Exiles
#12 jun 2002, #13 jul 2002 $3

Fantastic Four
#36 mar 1965 (cameo) $195
#73 apr 1968 $95
#133 apr 1973 (cameo) $25
#204 mar 1979 (cameo), #207 jun
1979 $6
#218 may 1980 $6
#242 may 1982, #243 jun 1982 $5
#250 jan 1983 52pages $7.50
#299 feb 1987, #336 jan 1990
(cameo), #347 dec 1990, #348 jan
1991,#349 feb 1991 $5
#362 mar 1992,#372 jan 1993,#373
feb 1993, #374 mar 1993, #375
apr 1993 (cameo),#378 jul 1993
                               $4
Volume 3
#2 feb 1998 (cameo), #7 jul 1998
(cameo), #9 sept 1998 $4
#22 oct 1999, #27 mar 2000 (2
pages), #36 dec 2000, #41 may
2001 $3
Annuals
#1 1963 $1,200
#3 1965 $200
#14 1979 (cameo) $7

#22 1989 $5
Felicia Hardy, The Black Cat
#1 jul 1994 $4
#4 oct 1994 $3
FoolKiller
#2 noc 1990 (cameo), #8 jun 1991
                               $2
Galactic Guardians
#1 jul 1994 (cameo) $4
Galactus The Devourer
#2 oct 1999 (cameo), #3 nov 1999,
#4 dec 1999 (cameo) $3
Generation X
#59 jan 2000 $3
Ghost Rider
#18 jun 1976 $15
Volume 2
#16 aug 1991, #17 sept 1991, #48
apr 1994 $3
Godzilla
#24 jul 1979 (1 page) $6
Guardians of the Galaxy
#54 nov 1994 $2.50
Annuals #3 1993 (cameo), #4 1994
(cameo) $3
**Impossible Man Summer Vacation
Spectacular** #1 1990 $2
Incredible Hulk
#277 nov 1982 (cameo), #278 dec
1982, #279 jan 1983, #300 oct
1984 $5
#349 nov 1988, #383 jul 1991
(cameo) $3
#467 aug 1998 $2.50
Incredible Hulk Annual #11 1982 $5
Infinity Crusade
#1 jun 1993 ($3.50 cover) $3.50
#2 jul 1993, #5 oct 1993, #6 nov
1993 ($2.50 cover) $2.50
Infinity Gauntlet
#1 jul 1991, #3 sept 1991, #4 oct
1991, #5 dec 1991
Infinity War #1
jun 1992, #2 jul 1992 ($2.50 cover)
                           $2.50
Iron Man
#234 sept 1988 $5

Journey into Mystery
#505 jan 1997 $2
Kazar #3
mar 1971 $25
Kazar the Savage
#21 dec 1982, #22 jan 1983, #23 feb
    1983, #24 mar 1983, #25 apr
    1983, #26 may 1983 $2
Longshot
#4 dec 1985 $5
Marvel Feature
#4 july 1972 $20
Marvel Fanfare
#1 mar 1982 $8
#2 apr 1982, #4 jun 1982 $6
#6 aug 1982 $4
#27 #42 $3
Volume 2
#3 nov 1996 $2
Marvel Heroes and Legends
#1 1996 ($2.95 cover) $3
Marvels
#2 feb 1994 (cameo), #3 mar 1994
    (cameo), #4 apr 1994, ($5.95
    cover) $7
#9 aug 1994 ($2.95 cover) $3
Marvel Super-Heroes
#14 may 1968 $75
Volume 2
#4 dec 1990 ($2.95 cover) $3
Marvel Tales - Reprints *Amazing
Spider-Man*
#1 – 1964 $395
#2 – 1965 More Spider-Man $125
#3 – 1966 $75
#4 jul\66, #5 sept\66 $40
#6 jan\67, #7 mar\67, #8 may\67, #9
    jul\67, #10 sept\67 $25
#11 nov\67, #12 jan\68, #13 mar\68,
    #14 may\68, #15 jul\68, #16
    sept\68, #17 nov\68, #18 jan\69,
    #19 mar\69, #20 may\69 $20
#21 jul\69, #22 sept\69, #23 nov\69,
    #24 jan\70, #25 mar\70, #26
    may\70, #27 jul\70, #28 oct\70,
    #29 jan\71, #30 apr\70, #31 jul\71,

#32 nov\71, #33 feb\71 (last
    double size 25¢ comic) $15
#34 jul\71 - #50 apr\74 $5
#51 jun\74 - #100 feb\79 $4
#101 mar\79 - #200 jun\87 $3
#201 jul\87 - 291 jun\94 $2.50
Spider-Man Appearances Only
Marvel Team Up
#1 mar\72 Human Torch, Sandman
                             $195
#2 may\72 Human Torch, Frightful
    Four $60
#3 jul\72 Mobius, Human Torch $60
#4 sept\72 X-Men $75
#5 nov\72 Vision, Puppet Master, #6
    jan\73 The Thing, Puppet Master,
    Mad Thinker, #7 mar\73 Thor,
    Kryllx, #8 apr\73 Cat, Man-Killer,
    #9 may\73 Iron Man, Tomorrow
    Man, #10 jun\73 Human Torch,
    Iron Man, Tomorrow Man $25
#11 jul\73 Inhumans, Maximus, Kang,
    #13 sept\73 Capt. America, Gray
    Gargoyle, #14 oct\73 Sub-Mariner
    #15 nov\73 Ghost Rider, #16
    dec\73 Capt. Marvel, #17 jan\74
    Mr. Fantastic, Moleman, #19
    mar\74 Kazar, #20 apr\74 Black
    Panther $15
#12 Aug\73 Werewolf $20
#21 may\74 Dr. Strange, #22 jun\74
    Hawkeye, #24 Brother jul\74
    Voodoo, #25 aug\74 Daredevil,
    #26 oct\74 Thor, #27 nov\74 Hulk,
    Chameleon, #28 dec\74 Hercules,
    #30 feb\75 Falcon $10
#31 mar\75 Iron Fist, #33 may\75
    Night Hawk, #34 jun\75 Valkyrie,
    #36 aug\75 Frankenstein, #37
    sept\75 Manwolf, #38 oct\75
    Beast, #39 nov\75 Human Torch,
    #40 dec\75 Suns Of The Tiger,
    Human Torch #41 jan\75 Scarlet
    Witch, #42 feb\76 Vision, #43
    mar\76 Dr. Doom, #44 apr\76
    Moondragon, #45 may\76 Kill-
    raven, #46 jun\76 Deathlok, #47

jul\76 Thing, #48 aug\76 Iron Man, #49 sept\76 Dr. Strange, Iron Man #50 oct\76 Iron Man, Dr. Strange, #51 nov\76 Iron Man, Dr. Strange, #52 dec\76 Capt. America, #54 feb\77 Hulk, #55 mar\77 Warlock, #56 apr\77 Daredevil, #57 may\77 Black Widow, #58 jun\77 Ghost Rider, #59 jul\77 Yellowjacket and The Wasp, #60 aug\77 Wasp $7
#53 jan\77 Hulk, (first Byrne X-Men) $35
#61 sept\77 Human Torch, #62 oct\77 Ms Marvel, #63 nov\77 Iron Fist, #64 dec\77 Daughters Of The Dragon, #65 jan\78 Capt. Britain, #66 feb\78 Capt. Britian, #67 mar\78 Tigra, #68 apr\78 Man-Thing, #69 may\78 Havok, #70 jun\78 Thor, #71 jul\78 Falcon, #72 aug\78 Iron Man, #73 sept\78 Daredevil, #74 oct\78 Not Ready For Prime Time Players, #75 nov\78 Power Man, #76 dec\78 Dr. Strange, #77 jan\79 Ms Marvel #78 feb\79 Wonder Man, #79 mar\79 Red Sonja, #80 apr\79 Dr. Strange and Clea, #81 may\79 Satana, #82 jun\79 Black Widow, #83 jul\79 Nick Fury, #84 aug\79 Master Of Kung Fu, #85 sept\85 Shang-chi, Black Widow, Nick Fury, #86 oct\79 Guardians Of The Galaxy, #87 nov\79 Blac Panther, #88 dec\80 Invisible Girl, #89 jan\80 Nightcrawler, #90 feb\80 Beast, #91 mar\80 Ghost Rider, #92 apr\80 Hawkeye, #93 may\80 Werewolf #94 jun\80 The Shroud #95 jul\80 Mockingbird, #96 aug\80 Howard the Duck, #98 oct\80 Black Widow, #99 nov\80 Machine Man $5
#100 dec\80 Fantastic Four $10
#101 jan\81 Nighthawk, #102 feb\81 DOC Samson, #103 mar\81 Ant-Man, #106 jun\81 Capt. America,

#107 jul\81 She Hulk, #108 aug\81 Paladin, #109 sept\81 Dazzler, #110 oct\81 Iron Man, #111 nov\81 Devil Slayer, #112 dec\81 King Kull, #113 jan\82 Quasar, #114 feb\82 Falcon, #115 mar\82 Thor, #116 apr\82 Valkyrie, #119 jul\82 Gargoyle, #120 aug\82 Dominic Fortune, #121 sept\82 Human Torch, #122 oct\82 Man Thing, #123 nov\82 Daredevil, #124 dec\82 Beast, #125 jan\83 Tigra, #126 feb\83 Hulk, #127 mar\83 Watcher, #128 apr\83 Capt. America, #129 may\83 vision, #130 jun\83 Scarlet Witch, #131 jul\83 Frogman, #132 aug\83 Mr. Fantastic, #133 sept\83 Fantastic Four, #134 oct\83 Jack Of Hearts, #135 nov\83 Kitty Pride, #136 dec\83 Wonder Man, #138 feb\84 Sandman, #139 mar\84 Nick Fury, #140 apr\84 Black Widow, #141 may\84 Daredevil (Spider-Man Black Costume), #142 Jun\84 Capt. Marvel, #143 jul\84 Starfox, #144 aug\84 Moon Knight, #145 sept\84 Iron Man, #146 oct\84 Nomad, #147 nov\84 Human Torch, #148 dec\84 Thor, #149 jan\85 Cannonball $3.50
#117 may\82 Wolverine, #118 jun\82 Professor X, Wolverine $5
#150 feb\1985 X-Men ($1.00 cover) $10

Annuals
#1 - 1976 X-Men $30
#2 - 1979 Hulk $10
#4 - 1981 Moonknight, Power Man, Iron Fist, Daredevil $7
#5 - 1982 Thing, Scarlet Witch, Dr Strange, Quasar, #6 - 1983 Cloak & Dagger, New Mutants, #7 - 1984 Alpha Flight $5

Marvel Team Up V II
#1 sept\97 Generation X ($1.99 cover) $3

#2 oct\97 Hercules, #3 nov\97 Sandman, #4 dec\97 Man Thing, #5 jan\98 Watcher, #6 feb\98 Namor, #7 mar\98 Blade $2

Marvel Two In One

#17 jul 1976 $8

#27 may 1977 $5

#69 nov 1980 (cameo), #90 aug 1982, #96 feb 1983 $3

Marvel Two In One Annual #2 1977 $20

Maximum Security #1 dec 2000 (cameo), #3 jan 2001 $3

Midnight Sons Unlimited #3 oct 1993 $4

Moon Knight, Marc Spector

#2 jul 1989 (cameo) $4

#19 oct 1990, #20 nov 1990, #21 dec 1990, #32 nov 1991, #33 dec 1991 $3

#57 dec 1993 $5

New Warriors

#32 feb 1993, #33 mar 1993, #34 apr 1993 $2.50

#59 may 1995,#61 jul 1995, #62 aug 1995, #63 sept 1995 #64 oct 1995, #65 nov 1995, #66 dec 1995, #67 jan 1996, #70 apr 1996, #71 may 1996 $2

Annuals #1 1991 (cameo), #2 1992, #3 1993 $3

Nova

#12 aug 1977, #15 nov 1977 $5

Volume2 #3 mar 1994 $2

Volume3 #5 sept 1999 $2

Out Law Kid #10 jun\72 $35

Peter Parker: Spider-Man

#1 jan\99 Ranger ($2.99 cover) $5

#2 feb\99 Thor, #3 Iceman, #4 Marrow, #5 Spider Woman #6 Kingpin, #7 Blade, Hunger, #8 Blade, Kingpin, Morbius, #10 Venom, #11 nov\99 Iron Man, Thor, Juggernaut #13 - #47 oct\02 Green Goblin $3

#12 dec\99 Sinister Six ($2.99 cover) $4

Annuals

1999 Man Thing ($3.50 cover) $4

2000 Bounty, Black Cat ($3.50 cover) $4

2001 Faire De Lain $3

Powerman and Iron Fist #125 sept\86 $2.75

Power Pack

#6 jan\85 $2.50

#21 apr\86 (cameo), #24 apr\87, #33 nov\87 $2.25

Punisher V2 #17 mar\97 $3

Punisher V4 #2 aug\01 $3

Punisher Kills The Marvel Universe, The #1 $7

Punisher War Journals

#14 jan\90, #15 feb\90 $5

#68 jul\94 $3

Quasar

#7 feb\90 $3

#24 jun\91, #60 jul\94 (cameo) $2.50

Questprobe #2 jan\95 $3

Rom

#23 oct\81 $5

#66 jul\85 $3

Ruins #2 sept\95 $5

Secret Defenders

#6 aug\93, #7 sept\93 #8 oct\93 $3

#25 mar\95 $2.50

Secret Wars

#1 may\84 $12

#2 jun\84, #3 jul\84, #4 aug\84 #5 sept\84 #6 oct\84 #7 nov\84 #9 jan\85, #10 feb\85 #11 mar\85 $8

#8 dec\84 1st - Alien Black Costume $35

#12 apr\85 $10

Volume 2 #2 aug\85, #8 feb\86, #9 mar\86 $4

Sentry

#3 nov\00, #4 dec\00, #5 jan\00 $3

Sentry-Spider-Man #1 feb\01 $3

Sentry VS The Void, The #1 feb\01 $3

Shadows & Light #2 apr\98 #3 jul\98 $3

Sensational She Hulk, The
#3 jul\89 $3
#29 jul\91, #37 mar\93 $2.50
Silver Surfer
#14 mar\70 $95
Volume 3
#52 aug\91, #54 Sept\91, #55 Sept\-
    91 (cameo in all) $4
#93 jun\93 $3
#128 may\97, #129 jun\97, #132
    oct\97 $2.50
Annual #2 1989 $4
Slapstick #1 nov\92(cameo), #2
dec\92 $2
Sleepwalker #5 oct\91, #6 nov\91,
    #17 oct\92 $2
Spectacular Spider-Man, The
(magazine)
#1 jul\68 Lo This Monster (B & W)
    40¢ cover $150

#2 Nov\68 Green Goblin (color)
    35¢ cover $150
Spectacular Spider-Man
#1 Dec\76 O - Spider-Man, Tarantula
                                                  $75
#2 jan\77 Kraven $25
#3 feb\77 Lightmaster $18
#4 Vulture, #5 Vulture #6 Human
    Torch, Morbius, #7 Morbius, #8
    Morbius, #9 White Tiger, #10
    sept\77 White Tiger $15
#11 oct\77 Inhumans, #12 Brother
    Power & Sister Sun, #13
    Razorback, #14 Razorback, #15
    Razorback, #16 Beetle, #17 Angle,
    Iceman, Rampage,#18 Angle,
    Iceman, Rampage, #19 Enforcers,
    #20 Lightmaster Enforcers, White
    Tiger, #21 Scorpion, #22 Moon
    Knight, Cyclone, #23 Moon

**Spectacular Spider-Man
Magazine 1**
Marvel Comics
Another incarnation of a *Spider-Man
Magazine.*

AIM giveaway
Marvel Comics
Special editions of comic book
giveaways are a good investment
because of limited availability.

Knight, Cyclone, #24 Hypno-Hustler, #25 Masked Marauder, White Tiger, 1st - Carrion and Tri-Man, #26 Daredevil $10

#27 feb\79 Masked Marauder, Tri-Man 1st Miller Daredevil $20

#28 mar\79 - #63 feb\82 $6

#64 mar\82 1st - Cloak & Dagger $14

#65 apr\82 - #68 #71 - #99 feb\85 $5

#69 apr\82 cloak & Dagger #70 Cloak & Dagger $8

#100 mar\85 Black Cat, Kingpin $7

#101 apr\85 - #199 apr\93 $4

#200 may\93 Green Goblin ($2.95 cover) $5

#201 jun\93 - #263 nov\98 $3

Annuals

#1 - 1979 Doctor Octopus $10

#2 - 1980 Rapier $6

#3 - 1981 Manwolf $5

#4 (1982) - #14 (1994) $4

Spider-Man

#1 aug\90 silver $8

#1 silver Spidy For ups code $6

#1 Silver Bagged $20

#1 Green $9

#1 Green Bagged $12

#1 Gold Edition 2nd printing $4

#1 Gold Edition Bagged ?

#1 Platinum Mailed to Retailers (10,000 copies) $150

#2 sept\90 Lizard $6

#3 oct\90 - #10 may\91 $5

#11 jun\91 - #49 aug\94 $4

#50 sept\94 Grim Hunter ($3.95 cover) $6

#50 Sept\94 ($2.50 cover), #57 apr\95 Scarlet Spider ($2.50 cover) $4

#51 oct\94 Gwen Stacy Clone ($2.95 cover), #54 jan\95 Scarlet Spider, Kaine, Grim Hunter ($2.75 cover) #57 apr\95 ($2.95 Cover, #65 feb\96 (bagged includes cas-

sette), #75 dec\96 Green Goblin ($2.95 cover) $5

#51 oct\94 - #53 dec\94, #55 feb\95, #56 mar\95, #58 may\95 - #74 nov\96, #76 - #97 nov\98 $3

#98 Mr. Fantastic, Green Goblin (Final Issue) $4

Annuals

1997 Marvel Zombie, Calypso $4

1998 Electra, Silencer $4

Spider-Man and Batman sept\95 (Marvel, DC) ($5.95 cover) $7

Spider-Man Team Up

#1 X-Men dec\95 ($2.95 cover) $4

#2 jan\96 Silver Surfer, #3 feb\96 Fantastic Four, #4 mar\96 Avengers, #5 apr\96 Gambit, Howard the Duck, #6 may\96 Dracula, #7 jun\96 Thunderbolts $3

Spidey Super Stories

#1 oct\74 Electro, Vulture $35

#2 nov\74 Kraven, Doc Octopus $20

#3 dec\74 Ringmaster $ His Circus Of Crime, #4 jan\75 Medusa, Beetle, #5 feb\75 Shocker $18

#6 mar\75 Iceman, #7 apr\75 Lizard, #8 may\75 Mole Man, #9 jun\75 Dr. Doom, Hulk, #10 Jul\75 Green Goblin $15

#11 aug\75 Doc Octopus, #12 sept\75 cat, owl, #13 nov\75 Falcon, Kraven, #14 dec\75 Shanna, #15 feb\76 Storm, #16 apr\76 Sub-Mariner, #17 jul\76 Capt. America, #18 aug\76 Kingpin, #19 oct\76 Silver Surfer, #20 dec\76 Human Torch, Invisible Girl $12

#21 feb\77 Doc Octopus, #22 apr\77 Ms Marvel, Beetle, #23 jun\77 Green Goblin, #24 jul\77 Thundra, #25 aug\77 Dr. Doom, #26 sept\77 Sandman, #27 oct\77 Loki, Thor, #28 nov\77 Medusa, #29 dec\77 Kingpin, #30 jan\78

Kang, Fantastic Four, #31 feb\78 Dr. Doom, #32 mar\78 Spider Woman #33 apr\78 Hulk, #34 may\78 Sub-Mariner, #35 jul\78 Shanna, #36 Sept\78 Lizard, #37 nov\78 White Tiger, #38 jan\79 Fantastic Four, #39 mar\79 Cat Thanos, #40 may\79 Hawkeye, #41 jul\79 Nova, Doc Octopus, #42 Sept\79 Kingpin, #43 nov\79 Daredevil, Ringmaster, #44 jan\80 Vision, Dr. Time, #45 mar\80 Silver Surfer, Dr. Doom, #46 may\80 Mysterio, #47 jul\80 Spider Woman, Stilt Man, #48 Sept\80 Green Goblin, #49 nov\80 Hawkeye, Jester, #50 jan\81 She Hulk, Rhino, #51 mar\81 Capt. America, Mad Thinker, #52 may\81 Human Torch, Mole Man, #53 jul\81 Sub-Mariner, Dr. Doom, #54 sept\81 Mr. Fantastic, Black Bolt, Madusa, #55 nov\81 Kingpin, #56 jan\82 Jack O'Lantern, Green Goblin. #57 mar\82 White Tiger, Trapster $10

Spirits of Vengeance #5 dec\92, #6 jan\92 $2

Strange Tales
#115 dec\63 $625
#119 apr\64 $135
#156 may\67 $65
Annual #2 sept\63 $1,200

Sub-Mariner
#14 jun\69 (cameo) $35
#40 aug\71 $15
#69 mar\73 $6

Supernaturals #1 dec\98 (cameo) $4

Tales to Astonish #57 jul\64 $250
Thing, The nov\83 $3
Thor
#233 mar\75 (cameo) $10
#271 may\78 (cameo) $8
#391 may\88 $5
#427 dec\90 (cameo), #447 may\92, #448 jun\92 $3

Volume2 #8 feb\99, #51 sept\02
                                  $2.50
Thunderbolts
#1 apr\97 (cameo) $10
#8 nov\97, #10 jan\98 (cameo) $4
Thunderbolts Life Sentences #1 jul\01 $4
Thunderstrike #4 jan\95, #5 feb\95, #6 mar\95 $2
Transformers #3 jan\85 $6
Vision and the Scarlet Witch V2 #11 aug\86 $2
Warlock #5 jan\00, #6 feb\00 $2
Warlock and the Infinity Watch #11 dec\92 $2
Web of Spider-Man
#1 Apr\85 Vulturions $25
#2 may\85 Vulturions, Kingpin $12
#3 jun\85 Vulturions, Kingpin, Vulture $10
#4 jul\85 Doc Octopus #5 aug\75 Doc Octopus #6 Sept\85 Kingpin #7 oct\85 Hulk #8 nov\85 Smithville Thunderbolt #9 dec\85 Smithville Thunderbolt, #10 jan\86 Dominic Fortune, Shocker $8
#11 feb\86 - #20 nov\86 $5
#21 dec\86 - #28 jul\87, #30 sept\87 #47 feb\89, #49 apr\89, #51 jun\89 - #60 jan\90 $4
#29 aug\87 Wolverine, Hobgoblin, #48 O – Hobgoblin $8
#61 jul\90 -#89 jun\92, #91 aug\91 - #99 Apr\93, #101 jun\93 - #112 may\94, #114 jul\94 - #116 sept\94, #118, #119, #121 feb\95 - #124 may\95, #126 jul\95 - #128 sept\95 $3
#90 Jul\92 Mysterio ($2.95 cover), #100 may\93 Spider Armor, Rose, Enforcers ($2.95 cover), #113 jun\94 Black Cat, Gambit ($2.95 bagged), #117 oct\94 Chameleon, Carnage (2.95 cover) $4
#120 jan\95 Scarlet Spider, Kaine, Grim Hunter $3.25

#125 jun\95 Scarlet Spider, Black Cat ($3.95 cover) $5

#129 oct\95 Scarlet Spider, Firestar, New Warriors $4

Annuals

#1 – 1985 $5

#2 - 1986 New Mutants, Hobgoblin $7

#3 (1987) - #10 (1994) $4

Web of Spider-Man Super Special

#1 - 1995 ($3.95 cover) $5

Wolverine #148 mar\00, #156 nov\00, #157 dec\00 $2.25

Wonderman #13 sept\92(cameo), #28 dec\93, #29 jan\94 $2

Worlds Greatest Comic Magazine

#3 apr\01 $3

X-Force #3 Oct\91, #4 nov\91 $2

X-Man

#24 feb\97, #26 apr\97 $3

#37 apr\98, #38 may\98,# 51 may\99(cameo) $2.50

X-Men

#27 dec\66 (cameo) $250

#35 Aug\67 $250

#83 aug\73 $75

#123 jul\79 $75

#135 jul\80 (cameo) $65

#190 feb\85, #191 mar\85 $10

#339 dec\96 (cameo), #346 aug\97 $4

X-Men Annual #14 1990 (cameo) 1st – Gambit $40

X-Men V2 #77 jul\98 $2

Internet Auctions

Here are some of the highest prices that were paid or bid (but which failed to meet a set reserve price) to buy key CGC graded books on Internet Auctions in 2002/2003. We are including these prices to show how much someone was willing to pay for a graded book:

Amazing Fantasy #15 CGC NM 9.4	$95,000
Amazing Spider-Man #1 CGC VF+ 8.5	$12,600
Amazing Spider-Man #1 CGC NM- 9.2	$17,600 (did not meet reserve)
Amazing Spider-Man #1 CGC NM 9.4	$67,305
Amazing Spider-Man #3 CGC VF+ 8.5	$2,750
Amazing Spider-Man #3 F\VF	$677 (not graded)
Amazing Spider-Man #5 CGC FN 6.0	$400
Amazing Spider-Man #6 CGC VF\NM 9.0	$1,925 (did not meet reserve)
Amazing Spider-Man #9 CGC NM+ 9.6	$2,500
Amazing Spider-Man #9 CGC NM+ 9.6	$3,000
Amazing Spider-Man #14 CGC VF- 7.5	$860
Amazing Spider-Man #14 CGC VG+ 4.5	$340
Amazing Spider-Man #17 CGC NM- 9.2	$1,750
Amazing Spider Man #23 CGC NM 9.4	$2,625

Amazing Spider-Man #24 CGC NM- 9.2	$600
Amazing Spider-Man #25 CGC VF 7.0	$175
Amazing Spider-Man #26 CGC NM- 9.2	$851.42 (did not meet reserve)
Amazing Spider-Man #28 CGC VF\NM 9.0	$500
Amazing Spider-Man #31 CGC VF\NM 9.0	$250
Amazing Spider-Man #32 CGC VF\NM 9.0	$250
Amazing Spider-Man #33 CGC VF\NM 9.0	$250
Amazing Spider-Man #39 & 40 both CGC NM+ 9.6	
Bid Price was $6,711 for both (did not meet reserve)	
Amazing Spider-Man #41 CGC VF+ 8.5	$250
Amazing Spider-Man #77 CGC NM 9.4	$251
Amazing Spider-Man #79 CGC NM 9.4	$307.57
Amazing Spider-Man #81 CGC NM 9.4	$227.50
Amazing Spider-Man #95 CGC NM 9.4	$230.51
Amazing Spider-Man #100 CGC NM+ 9.6	$760
Amazing Spider-Man #100 CGC VF\NM	$300
Amazing Spider-Man Annual #1 VF	$560 (not graded)
Aquaman #1 CGC NM- 9.2	$1,982.77 (did not meet reserve)
Captain America Comics #1 VF+ 8.5	$95,000
Daredevil #1 CGC NM- 9.2	$6,300
Daredevil #1 CGC VF\NM 9.0	$3,370
Daredevil #2 CGC NM- 9.2	$1,924
Fantastic Four #1 NM- 9.2	$37,500
Fantastic Four #3 CGC NM+ 9.6	$8,000.99
Fantastic Four #4 CGC 8.0 VF\ NM	$1,575
Fantastic Four #5 CGC NM 9.2	$9,400 (did not meet reserve)
Fantastic Four #48 CGC NM+ 9.6	$2,100
Iron Man #1 CGC NM+ 9.6	$999.99
Iron Man #1 CGC NM+ 9.6	$1,009
Journey into Mystery #88 CGC NM 9.4	$4,799
Marvel Comics #1 CGC VF\NM 9.0	$350,000
Showcase #4 CGC NM- 9.2	$55,200 (did not meet reserve)
Showcase #4 CGC NM- 9.2	$91,677.77 (did not meet reserve)
	(not same book as above)
Showcase #9 CGC VF+ 8.5	$4,700 (did not meet reserve)
Showcase $34 CGC Vf+ 8.5	$1,200
Spider-Man (silver 1990) CGC M 9.9	$101 (did not meet reserve)
Strange Tales #110 CGC NM 9.4	$7,050.99 (did not meet reserve)
Superman's Girl Friend Lois Lane F\VF	$1,124 (not graded)
X-Men #1 CGC VF\NM 9.0	$9,601.99

Chapter 12:
Price Guide

Notes

See pricing legend in previous chapter.

Our pricing focuses on general distribution comic books (e.g. does not include limited additional covers that which were never in the primary distribution channel)

Action Comics
DC (1938–Present)

1 1st Superman	$325,000
2	$40,000
3	$25,000
4	$17,000
5	$15,000
6	$15,000
7 2nd Superman Cover	$22,000
200, 201	$495
202–220	$425
221–250	$350
242 1st Brainiac, City of Kandor, Origin Brainiac	$2,500
250, 251	$250
252 1st, O Supergirl	$2,750
253 2nd Supergirl	$595
254 1st Bizarro, Superman	$395
255 1st Bizarro, Lois Lane	$325
256–266, 268–270	$225
271–275, 277–282 (last 10¢ issue)	$195

276 1st Phantom Girl, Shrinking Violet, Sunboy	$250
283–299	$150
300	$175
301– 333, 335–340	$75
334 GS	$95
341–346, 348–359, 361–372, 374–378 last 12¢ comic 379-399	$40
347, 360, 373 GS	$75
400–413	$35
414–418, 420–424	$15
419 1st Human Target	$18
425 Nadams	$25
426–431, 433–436, 438–440 (440 1st Grell, Green Arrow)	$12
432 1st SA Toyman	$25
437, 443 GS	$40
441, 442 Mike Grell, Green Arrow	$10
443 Justice League	$12
444–448, 450–499	$8
449 GS	$20
500 Superman Story Infinite Cover	$12
501–599	$5
600 50th Anniversary issue, Various artists	$8
601–699	$4
700 regular edition	$5
700 platinum	$20
701–774	$3
775 double size	$3.75
776 up	$2.50
Annuals	
1 Aadams, Jbyr Batman	$4
2–9	$3

Adventure Comics
DC (1938–1983)

40 jul\39 Sandman	$60,000
48 1st Hourman	$34,000
61 1st Starman	$18,000
72 1st Simon/Kirby Sandman,	
73 O – Manhunter	$15,000
200 may\54	$750
201–209, 211–213, 215–220	$395
210 1st Krypto	$4,500
214 2nd App Krypto	$595
221–246, 248–250	$325
247 1st Legion of Superheroes	
	$7,500
251–255, 257–259, 261–266, 268,	
270, 272–274	$195
256 Jack Kirby, O Green Arrow	
	$925
260 Origin Silver Age Aquaman	
	$1,000
267 2nd App Legion of Superheroes	
	$1,200
269 1st, O Aqualad	$350
271 O (retold) Lex Luthor	$350
275 O Superman, Batman Team Up	
	$250
276–281, 284, 287–289	$175
282 1st, O Starboy, 5th Legion	$295
283 1st Phantom Zone	$250
285 1st Bizarro World	$225
286 1st Bizarro Mzyzptik	$200
290 Legion app O Sunboy	
(last 10¢ issue)	$250
291, 292, 294–299	$150
293 Legion, 1st Legion of Super Pets	
	$210
300	$500
301 O Bouncing Boy	$200
302–310	$125
311–330	$95
331–350	$75
351–380 (last 12¢ issue)	$60
381 Supergirl	$100
382–389, 391–399	$30

390, 403 80pp	$50
400 Anniversary issue	$40
401–402, 404–408	$20
409–420	$30
421–427, 429, 430	$15
428 1st Black Orchid	$50
431 Birth Spectre	$75
432–440 Spectre	$30
441–460, 463–467	$10
461–462 Batman Earth–2 GS	$30
468–490	$5
491–503 GS	$10
GS 1	$5

ALIAS
Max/Marvel (2001)

1	$4
2–3	$3

Angel
Dark Horse (1999–2001)

1A Regular Cover	$4
1B Photo Cover	$5
2A Regular Cover	$3
2B Photo Cover	$4
3–17 Regular Covers	$3

Aliens
Dark Horse (1986–1989)

1 1st	$20
2	$8
3–6	$5

Aquaman
DC (1962–1977)

1	$1,250
2	$400
3	$325
4–10	$225
11–20	$175
21–32, 34–40	$75
33	$95
41–49	$50
50–52 Deadman Nadams	$75
53–57	$25

Atom, The
DC (1962–1968)

1	$1,250

2	$450	57 1st Vision	$135
3, 7	$350	58 O Vision	$75
4–6, 8–10	$250	59 1st Yellowjacket	$40
11–20	$125	60–70	$35
21–28, 30–40	$75	71 1st Invaders	$60
29 GA Atom	$195	72–86, 88–92, 97–99	$30

Astro City
Image Mini-series (1995–1996)

		87 O Black Panther	$45
1	$15	93 Nadams art	$75
2 $12		94–96 Nadams art	$60
3–6	$10	100	$125

Astro City
Image/Homage Series (1996–1998)

		101–109, 112–140, 144	$15
		110, 111 X-Men	$40
1	$7	141–143, 145–200	$5
2–5	$7	202–402	$4
6–15	$4	Annuals	

DC/Homage Series (1999–Present)

		1	$105
16–22	$3	2	$50

The Authority
DC/Wildstorm (1999–Present)

		3	$40
		4, 5	$25
1	$15	7–9	$10
2	$10	10 1st Rogue	$45
3–5	$7	11–23	$5
6–10	$6	GIANT SIZES	
11, 12	$5	1–5	$12
13	$7		

Babylon 5
DC (1995)

14–23	$4	1	$18
24 up	$3	2	$12

Avengers
Marvel (1963–1996)

		3–5	$8
		6–11	$6

Batgirl
DC (2000–Present)

1 1st	$4,200	1	$5
2 1st Mansion	$950	2–5	$3
3 Hulk versus Sub-Mariner	$595	6 up	$2.50
4 Re–enter SA Captain America			

Batman
DC (1940–Present)

	$2,500	1 1st Joker app	$125,000
5 1st Lava Men	$395	5 1st Batmobile	$7,200
6 1st Masters of Evil	$320	16 1st Alfred	$7,900
7–10	$295	49 1st Mad Hatter	$2,000
11 Spider-Man App	$325	92 1st BatHound	$850
12–15, 17–20	$150	100 jun\56	$3,000
16 Original team quits	$195	101 Clark Kent	$595
21–52	$50		
53 X-Men	$65		
54–56	$45		

102–104, 106–110	$500	400 Stephen King story	$25
105 Bat Woman	$675	401–403, 405–416	$10
111–120	$395	404 Miller Year 1	$15
121 1st Mr. Freeze	$525	417–420 Ten nights of beast	$12
122–128,130	$325	421–425, 429–450	$5
129 O Robin retold	$395	426–428 Death in the family	$18
131–143 (last 10¢ issue)	$295	451–499	$4
144–150	$225	500	$5
151–154, 156–168, 170	$175	501 up	$3
155 1st SA Penguin	$500	Annuals	
169 2nd Penguin	$225	1 1961	$1000
171 1st SA Riddler	$675	2, 3	$400
172–175, 177, 178, 180	$125	4–7	$195
176	$200	8–10	$10
182,185,187,193,198 GS	$175	11 up	$4

Batman: Gotham Knights
DC (2000–Present)

181 1st Poison Ivy	$295	1	$3
183 2nd Poison Ivy	$160	2–10	$2.50
184–186, 188, 190–192, 194–197,		11	$3.25
199	$95	12 up	$2.50
189 1st SA Scarecrow	$195		

Batman: Legends of the Dark Knight
DC (1989–Present)

200 Nadams	$225	1–148	
201, 202, 204–207, 209–212		149 up	
(last 12¢ issue)	$50		

Batman: Shadow of the Bat
DC (1992–2000)

203, 208, 218, 223, 228, 233 GS	$75	1	$5
213 O Alfred, Robin GS	$125	2–10	$4
214–217, 220–222, 224–226,		11–99	$3
229–231	$40	100	$4
219 Nadams	$65	101 up	$2.50

Batman: The Dark Knight Returns
DC (1996)

227 Nadams	$50	1 Miller	$30
232 1st Ra's Al Ghul	$175	2 Miller	$20
234 1st SA Two–Face	$225	3 Miller	$15
235–236, 239–242, 246–250	$35	4 Miller	$15

Battle Chasers
Image/Cliffhanger (1998)

237, 251 Nadams art	$95	1	$10
238 100pg	$75	2–4	$5
243–245 Nadams	$60		
252, 253, 263–300	$25		
254, 256–259, 261	$60		
255 100pg Nadams	$75		
260 100pg	$75		
262 GS	$45		
301–350	$18		
351–356, 358–365, 367–399	$12		
357 1st Jason Todd	$15		
366 J. Todd in Robin costume	$20		

DC/Cliffhanger (1999–2001)		34 1st, O SA Hawkman	$3,200
5–8	$3	35 Hawkman	$750
Image Comics		36 Hawkman	$600
9	$3.50	37–39 Suicide Squad	$250
Birds of Prey		40–41 C. Carson	$200
DC (1998–Present)		42, 44 Hawkman	$400
1	$5	43 O retold Hawkman	$500
2, 3	$3	45–49	$75
4 up	$2.50	50–53	$150
Black Panther		54 1st, O Teen Titans	$400
Marvel (1977–1979)		55, 56, 58, 59	$125
1	$25	57 1st Metamorpho	$225
2	$15	60 1st Wonder Girl	$125
3–15	$10	61,62 Origin Starman	$150
Volume 2 (1998–Present)		63–86	$75
1	$5	87–99	$45
2	$3	100	$65
3–10	$2.75	101	$25
11 up	$2.50	102 Nadams	$35
Blade		103–110	$20
Marvel (1998–1999)		111, 118	$25
1	$4	112–117 100pg	$50
2, 3	$3	119–141	$15
Brave & the Bold		142–199	$8
DC (1955–1983)		200 1st Outsiders	$12
1 1st Viking Prince	$5,200	*Brotherhood, The*	
2	$1,800	Marvel (2001–Present)	
3	$900	1	$3
4	$750	2	$2.50
5 Robin Hood Starts	$850	3 up	$2.25
6–10	$500	*Buffy the Vampire Slayer*	
11–22	$400	Dark Horse (1998–Present)	
23 Origin Viking Prince	$600	1 regular photo cover	$10
24	$350	2 regular photo cover	$6
25 1st Suicide Squad	$625	3–10 regular photo covers	$5
26 SS	$400	11–20 regular photo covers	$4
27 SS	$350	21 up	$3
28 1st Justice League of America		Annuals	
	$8,500	1999	$5
29 JLA	$3,500	*Buffy the Vampire Slayer: OZ*	
30 JLA	$2,750	Dark Horse (2001)	
31 1st Cave Carson	$500	1–3 photo/regular covers	$4
32 C. Carson	$300	*Cage*	
33 C. Carson	$250	Marvel (1992–1993)	

1	$4	2		$60
2, 3	$3	3, 4		$40
4–11, 13–20	$2.50	5–10		$25
12 king size, Iron Fist App	$4	11–14 last 12¢ issue		$20

Captain America
Marvel (1968–1996)

100 (takes up where Tales of Suspense left off)	$450	15–24	$12
101, 109 (O retold)	$125	25 Jim Starlin art starts	$28
102–108	$95	26 Starlin	$25
110 1st Viper	$105	27–36	$12
111–115	$70	37–62	$8

Volume 2 (1995–1996)

117 1st Falcon	$95	1	$3
118–136, 139, 140	$20	2–6	$2

Volume 3 (1999–Present)

137–138 Spiderman app	$25	1	$3
141, 142, 144–171	$15	2 up	$2.50

Catwoman
DC Mini-series (1989)

172–175 Original X-Men App	$18	1–4	$10

Series (1993–2001)

176–199	$12	1	$5
200	$15	2–10	$4
201–240	$10	11–94	$3

Annuals

241 Punisher App	$15	1–4	$3

Cerebus
Aardvark–Vanaheim (1977–Present)

242–246, 256–300	$5	1	$300
247–255 Byrne art	$8	1 counterfeit (inside cover glossy)	
301–454	$4	2,3	$95

Annuals

1 1971	$50	4–6	$65
2 1972	$30	7–10	$50
3,4 1976–77	$20	11–20	$20
5–7, 9–13	$5	21	$40
8 Wolverine App	$20	22–30	$12

Volume 2 (1996–1997)

1 Leifield	$5	31–50	$8
2	$4	51–100	$6
3–11, 13	$3	101–160, 161–200	$4
12 ($2.99 cover)	$4	161 Bone	$10

Volume 3 (1997–Present)

1	$8	201 up	$2.50

Crisis on Infinite Earths
DC (1985–1986)

2	$5	1 Wolfman & Perez	$20
3–11, 12–20	$4	2–6	$12
12 ($2.99 cover)	$5	7 D Supergirl	$25
21 up	$3		

Captain Marvel
Marvel (1968–1979)

1	$150

8 D Flash	$30		255–379	$3
9–11	$10		Annuals	
12 GS	$12		1 1967	$75

Crossgen Chronicles
Crossgen Comics (2000–Present)

1 up	$4		2, 3 1971–72	$25
			4 1976	$10
			5–10	$4

Daredevil
Marvel (1964–1988)

Volume 2 (1998–Present)
"Marvel Knights"

1	$3,800		1	$10
2 Electro App	$750		2	$7
3	$550		3–10	$4
4	$395		11–26	$3
5	$275		27 up	$2.75
6	$225			

Daredevil
Marvel Mini-series (1993)

7 1st red costume, Sub-Mariner	$400		1 Miller	$5
8–10	$195		2–5 Miller	$4

11–15	$125	

The Darkness
Top Cow (1996–Present)

16–17 Spider-Man App in both	$150		1	$10
18 1st Gladiator	$125		2, 3	$7
19–20	$95		4–10	$5
21–30	$75		11–40	$2.75
31–40, 43–53 (last 12¢ issue)	$45		41 up	$2.50
41 D Mike Murdock, 42 1st Jester				
	$50			

Dawn
Sirius (1995–1996) regular edition

54–76, 78–79	$28		1	$8
77 Spider-Man App	$30		2	$5
80–99	$20		3–6	$3
100	$40			

Defenders, The
Marvel (1972–1986)

101–120	$15		1 Hulk, Dr. Strange, Sub-Mariner	
121–130, 132–140	$12			$150
131 1st, O Bullseye	$40		2	$75
141–157	$10		3–5	$50
158 Miller story and art	$50		6–9	$30
159 Miller story and art	$35		10 Thor VS Hulk	$40
160–161 Miller story and art	$25		11–14, 17–20	$18
162 Ditko art	$8		15, 16 Magneto, Prof. X	$25
163–167	$20		21–50	$9
168 1st Electra, Miller story and art			51–99	$5
	$65		100	$7
169–180, 182–184 Punisher	$10		101–152	$3
181 GS D Electra	$20			
185–200, 250 1st Bullet	$5			
201–249, 251–253, 380	$4			
254 1st Typhoid Mary	$10			

Annual		437 Manhunter	$50
1 $1976	$20	438–445 100pp	$75
Volume 2 (2001–Present)		446–465	$20
1	$4	466–468	$35
2	$3	469–470	$25
3–10	$2.50	471–474, 479	$30
11 up	$2.25	475–476	$50
Detective		477 Nadams	$28
DC (1937–Present)		480 44pp	$22
1	$125,000	481–495	$25
2	$28,000	496–499	$12
3	$20,000	500	$20
27 1st Batman	$325,000	501–523	$8
33 O Batman	$60,000	524–525 Jason Todd	$12
38 1st Robin	$50,000	526 500th App in series	$20
100 jun\45	$2,000	527–574	$6
200 jan\53	$950	575–578 Year Two	$15
201–204, 206–210	$600	579–599	$4
205 O Batcave	$1,000	600	$5
211–224	$500	601–700	$3
225 1st Martian Manhunter	$8,200	701 up	$2.50
226 O Martian Manhunter	$2,100	Annuals	
227–229	$600	1 1988	$5
230 1st Mad Hatter	$750	2–10	$3
231, 232, 234, 237–240	$425	*Earth X*	
233 1st, O Batwoman	$2,000	Marvel (1999–2000)	
235 O Batman's Costume	$850	1	$5
336	$495	2–12	$3
241–262	$360	*Electra*	
263–264, 266, 268–273	$275	Marvel (2001–Present)	
265 Batman O retold	$400	1	$6
267 1st,O BatMite	$450	2	$4
274–297 last 10¢ issue	$195	3 up	$3
298 1st new Clayface	$350	*The Establishment*	
299–320	$125	DC/Wildstorm (2001–Present)	
321–326, 329–358, 360–368	$75	1	$3
327, 328 D Alfred	$150	2 up	$2.50
359 1st, O modern Batgirl	$195	*Evil Ernie*	
369 Nadams	$95	Eternity/Chaos! Comics	
370–388 last 12¢ issue	$65	(1991–1992)	
391–399	$50	1 1st Evil Ernie, 1st Lady Death	$75
400 1st Man–Bat, Nadams	$95	2–4	$30
401–424	$40	5	$20
425–436	$30		

Exiles, The
Marvel (2001–Present)

1	$3
2–6, up	$2.50

Fantastic Four
Marvel (1961–1996)

1 1st, O F.F., Stan Lee, Jack Kirby start	$35,000
1B Golden Record Rep with no cover price	$200
1C Golden Record Rep with record	$300
2 1st Scrulls last 10¢ issue	$6,200
3	$4,000
4 1st SA Sub-Mariner	$4,900
5 1st, O Dr. Doom	$6,000
6 Doom, Sub-Mariner	$2,500
7	$1,350
8 1st Puppet Master	$1,500
9,10	$1,300
11 1st Impossible Man	$1,000
12 1st Hulk VS Thing	$1,950
13 1st Watcher	$750
14, 16, 17, 19	$475
15 1st Mad Thinker	$500
18 1st Super Scrull	$500
20 1st Molecule Man	$500
21–24, 27, 29, 30	$300
25–26 Hulk	$595
28 X-Men App	$450
31 1st Dr. Franklin Storm	$195
32, 33–35, 37–43	$135
33 1st Attuma	$195
36 1st Medusa, 1st Frightful Four	$195
44 1st Gorgon	$150
45 1st Crystal, 1st Black Bolt	$195
46 1st Inhumans	$140
47	$125
48 1st Silver Surfer, 1st Galactus	$1,750
49 Silver Surfer, Galactus	$500
50 Silver Surfer, Galactus	$475
51	$110
52 1st Black Panther	$250
53 1st Klaw	$175
54	$110
55 Silver Surfer	$150
56 Silver Surfer	$110
57 Silver Surfer, Dr. Doom	$100
58–65	$85
66 O Him/Adam Warlock	$150
67 Him /1st Warlock	$175
68–71	$75
72, 77, Silver Surfer, 73 Spider-Man	$95
74–76, 78–83	$65
84–88 last 12¢ issue	$55
89–99	$50
100	$150
101,105–111	$50
102–104	$50
112 Hulk VS Thing	$125
113–114	$35
115 1st Eternals last 15¢ issue	$40
116 52pp	$45
117–120	$30
121–123	$40
124–149	$25
150 Crystal and Quicksilver's wedding	$35
151–163	$15
164 1st Frankie Raye	$15
165–167 George Perez art ,168	$12
169–199	$8
200	$12
201–208	$6
209 1st H.E.R.B.I.E. the robot, Jbyr art	$8
210–231	$6
232 Jbyr story, art	$10
233–249, 251–350	$5
250 52pp	$7.50
351–416	$4

Annuals

1 1963	$1,200
2 1964	$500
3 Reed and Sue married 1965	$200

4 Original Human Torch app 1966		152–159, 161–168,170	$125
	$150	160 80pp	$160
5 Silver Surfer 1967	$150	169 80pp	$150
6 1968	$100	171–174	$95
7 1969	$50	175 Flash VS Superman	$250
8–10	$25	176–177, 179–186, 188, 189	
11–15	$10	last 12¢ issue	$75
16–20	$7	178 80pp	$125
21–27	$5	187 68pp	$95
Giant–Size		190–195, 197–199	$60
2–6	$20	196 68pp	$80
Volume 2 (1996–1997)		200	$60
1	$5	201–204	$40
2–11, 13	$4	205 80pp	$65
12 $2.99 cover	$5	206–207	$35
Volume 3 (1997–Present)		208–213	$45
1	$7	214 100pp	$75
2	$5	215 52pp	$50
3–10	$4	216	$30
11 up	$3	217–219 Nadams	$40
Flash		220	$25
DC (1959–1985)		221–225	$20
105	$7,500	226 Nadams	$25
106	$2,500	227–228	$18
107	$1,200	229, 232 100pp	$50
108	$1,000	230–231, 233–250	$15
109	$700	251–288, 290	$10
110 1st, O Kid Flash	$2,100	289 1st George Perez art at DC	
111	$600		$12
112 1st Elongated Man	$700	291–350	$6
113 1st Trickster	$575	Annuals	
114 Captain Cold	$425	1 1963	$650
115, 116, 118–121	$350	Volume 2 (1987–Present)	
117 1st Captain Boomerang	$425	1	$20
122 1st top	$375	2	$8
123 1st Earth-2, GA Flash	$2,100	3–10	$6
124 last 10¢ issue	$300	11–30	$5
125–128,130	$225	31–91, 63–99	$4
129 GA Flash,	$425	92 1st Impulse	$6
131–136, 138–140	$175	100	$6
137 GA Flash, JSA (cameo)	$500	101–175	$3
141–150	$150	176 up	$2.50
151 GA Flash	$195	Annuals	
		1–13	$4

Fray
Dark Horse (2001–Present)

1	$5
2	$4
3–5	$3

Gen13
Image/Wildstorm (1995–1998)

1	$5
2–36	$4

DC/Wildstorm (1999–Present)

37 up	$3

Ghost Rider
Marvel (1973–1983)

1	$100
2	$45
3–10	$30
11–19	$15
20 Daredevil	$20
21–30	$8
31–81	$5

Volume 2 (1990–1998)

1	$5
2, 3	$4
4–10	$3.50
11–93	$3

Annuals

1–2	$4

Volume 3 (2000–Present)

1	$4
2 up	$3

GI Joe
Marvel (1982–1994)

1 Baxter Paper, Television tie-in	$22
2	$17
3–20	$12
21 1st Storm Shadow	$14
22–50	$8
51–92	$6
93	$10
94–96	$5
97–149	$4
150–154	$10
155	$15

Image (2001)

1	$5
2 up	$3

Green Arrow
DC Mini-series (1983)

1–4	$5

Volume 1 (1988–1998)

1	$8
2–20	$4
21–99	$3
100 holographic foil cover	$7
101 D Oliver Queen	$18
102–136	$3
137	$7

Annuals

1–7	$4

Volume 2 (2001–Present)

1	$12
2	$6
3	$4
4 up	$2.50

Green Lantern
DC (1960–1986)

1 O retold 1st Guardians	$5,500
2 1st Pieface	$1,200
3	$700
4	$475
5 1st H. Hammond	$495
6	$400
7 1st, O Sinestro	$375
8, 9 last 10¢ issue	$325
10–12, 14, 15	$275
13 Flash	$300
16 1st, O Star Sapphire	$250
17–19	$225
20 Flash	$250
21–30	$195
31–36, 38, 39	$150
37 1st Evil Star	$160
40 1st GA Green Lantern	$700
41, 42, 44, 46–50	$125
45 GA Green Lantern	$200
51	$100
52 GA Green Lantern	$150

53–58, 60	$95	**Volume 2 (1986–1990)**	
59 1st Guy Gardner	$295	1	$10
61 G.A Green Lantern	$110	2	$6
62–69 last 12¢ issue	$95	3–12	$5
70–75	$50	13–19	$4
76 Nadams Green Arrow	$300	20–40	$3
77 Nadams GA	$100	***Harley Quinn***	
78 Nadams GA	$75	DC (2000–Present)	
79–84 Nadams GA	$60	1	$6
85–86 Nadams Drugs	$95	2–10	$4
87 Nadams	$50	11–20 up	$3
88	$25	***HellBlazer***	
89 Nadams	$50	DC/Vertigo (1988–Present)	
90–99	$15	1 John Constantine	$20
100 GS	$20	2	$12
101–111	$10	3–5	$10
112 GA/Green Lantern O retold	$20	6–8, 10–20	$6
113–115	$8	9, 19 Sandman	$8
116 Guy Gardner App as GL	$50	27 scarce	$20
117–140	$6	28–40	$4
141 1st Omega Men	$8	41 1st Garth Ennis work	$6
142–199	$4	42–160	$3
200	$5	161 up	$2.50
Volume 2 (1990–Present)		Annuals	
1	$10	1 1989	$10
2	$6	***Hulk, The***	
3–10	$5	Marvel (1999)	
11–45	$4	1 Jbyr	$8
46 Reign of Supermen	$8	2	$5
47	$4	3–7	$4
48 1st Kyle Rayner	$8	8 Wolverine App	$6
49	$7	9–11	$3
50 1st Kyle Rayner as Green Lantern		***Hulk Smash***	
	$10	Marvel (2001)	
51–80	$3.50	1 Marvel Knights	$5
81	$6	2	$4
82–99	$3	***Hunter: The Age of Magic***	
100	$7.50	DC/Vertigo (2001–Present)	
101–107	$3	1	$4
107 up	$2.50	2–6	$3
Grendel		***Iceman***	
Comico (1983–1984)		Marvel Mini-series (2001)	
1	$150	1	$4
2–3	$100	2–4	$3

Incredible Hulk
Marvel (1962–1963)

1 1st, O Hulk, 1st Rick Jones	$21,000
2	$4,500
3	$2,800
4	$2,500
5	$2,200
6	$3,200

Incredible Hulk (Marvel)
(Hulk appears in *Tales to Astonish*)
Volume 2 (1968–1999)

102 O retold	$400
103	$195
104	$175
105 1st Missing Link	$125
106–108	$95
109–110	$85
111–117 last 12¢ issue	$75
118–121	$50
122 versus Thing	$80
123–126	$40
127–140	$30
141 1st, O Doc Samson	$60
142–144	$20
145 O retold	$35
146–161	$18
162 1st Wendigo	$30
163–171,173–176	$15
172 O Juggernaut retold	$30
177 D Adam Warlock	$20
178	$18
179	$12
180 Wolverine (cameo)	$150
181 1st full Wolverine	$1,200
182 Wolverine	$140
183–199	$12
200	$30
201–249	$8
250 Silver Surfer, Giant	$12
251–313	$5
314–323	$6
324 Grey Hulk	$15
325 1st Hulk II	$6
326–329	$4

330 Todd McFarlane art	$30
331 Todd McFarlane art	$25
332–334 Todd McFarlane art	$20
335–339	$3
340 Todd McFarlane art, Wolverine App	$40
341–346 Todd McFarlane art	$10
347–366	$3
367 1st Dale Keown	$6
368–371	$3
372	$5
373–449	$3
449 1st Thunderbolts	$8
450	$6
451–473	$2.50
474 last issue	$5

Annuals

1 1968	$150
2 1969	$85
3–4, 71–72	$35
5–8	$20
9–11	$5
12–20	$3

Volume 3 (2000–Present)

12–23	$4
24–34 up	$2.50

Invaders, The
Marvel (1975–79)

1	$50
2	$28
3–6, 8–10	$20
7 1st Union Jack O Human Torch retold	$25
11–20	$15
21–30	$12
31–40	$10
41 GS last issue	$15

Annuals

1 1977	$25

Iron Man
Marvel (1968–1996)

1 O Iron Man story line continued from Iron Man and Sub #1	$800
2	$250

3–10	$125	85 1st Loki	$1,200	
11–15 last 12¢ issue	$75	86 1st Odin	$750	
16–24	$50	87–90	$500	
25 Sub-Mariner	$60	91–96	$300	
26–30	$40	97 1st Lava Man	$250	
31–40	$30	98 1st, O Human Cobra	$250	
41, 42, 44–46, 48–50	$20	99 1st Surtur and Mr. Hyde	$275	
43 1st Guardsman 52pp	$35	100	$275	
47 O Iron Man Barry Smith	$28	101 Avengers	$200	
51–53 Starlin	$20	102–108,110	$175	
54 1st Moondragon, Sub-Mariner		109 Magneto	$225	
	$35	111, 113, 115–125	$150	
55 1st Thanos (cameo) Starlin		112 Hulk, O Loki	$350	
cover/art	$100	114 1st, O Absorbing Man	$175	
56 Starlin	$25	126 Title Becomes Thor	$275	
57–75	$15	127–130	$125	
76–99	$12	131–140	$95	
100	$35	141–157	$75	
101–200	$7	158 O retold	$100	
201–300	$5	159–164, 167	$50	
301–331	$3	165 1st full Warlock last12¢ issue		
332	$5		$100	
Annuals		166 Warlock	$60	
1 1970	$50	168, 169 O Galactus	$75	
2 1971	$25	170–181, (180, 181) Nadams	$60	
3, 4 1976–77	$15	182–192	$35	
5–11 1982–94	$5	193 Silver Surfer 52pp	$75	
JLA		194–200	$25	
DC (1997–Present)		201–250	$15	
1	$25	251–300	$8	
2	$15	301–336, 338–383, 385–399	$5	
3–5	$10	337 Bata Ray Bill becomes Thor	$10	
6–10	$7	384 New Thor (Dargo)	$7	
11–20	$6	400 68pp	$7	
21–30	$5	401–410	$4	
31–41	$4	411 68pp	$6	
42–50	$3	412 1st full New Warriors	$8	
51 up	$2.50	413–449, 451–481, 483–499, 501	$3	
Journey into Mystery		450, 482, 500	$4	
Marvel (1962–1998)		502 last issue	$5	
83 1st Thor	$7,200	Annuals		
83 1966 reprint	$175	1 1965 Journey into Mystery	$295	
with record	$250	2 1966	$150	
84	$1,600	3,4 1971	$50	

5–8 1976–79	$20	61–63, 65, 66, 68–72 last 12¢ issue	
9, 10 1981–82	$10		$95
11–19 1983–94	$5	64 1st SA Red Tornado	$110
Justice League		67 GS	$125
DC (1987–1996)		73–75, 77–80	$75
1	$12	76 GS	$95
2	$7	81–84, 86–90	$45
3–10	$5	85, 93 GS	$75
11–50	$3	91, 92, 95–99 52pp	$70
51–68, 70–113	$2.50	94 1st, O Sandman and Starman	
69 Doomsday story	$7	(reprints)	$125
Justice League of America		100	$75
DC (1960–1987)		101, 102 JSA	$45
1 1st Desrero	$7,200	103–109	$35
2	$2,100	110–116 100pp	$60
3 1st, O Kanjar Ro	$1,500	117–120	$25
4 Green Arrow Joins The JLA	$1,000	121–157	$20
5 1st, O Dr. Destiny	$725	158–170	$12
6	$650	171–199	$8
7 last 10¢ issue	$575	200	$10
8	$500	201–260	$5
9 O Justice League	$1,200	261 last issue	$10
10 1st, O Felix Faust	$695	*Married with Children*	
11, 13, 15–20	$395	Now Comics (1990–1991)	
12 1st, O Dr. Light	$425	1, 2	$3
14 Atom Joins JLA	$425	3–7	$2.50
21 1st JSA, 1st SA App Dr. Fate and		Volume 2	
Hourman	$700	1, 4, 5, 9	$3
22 JSA Story cont.	$500	2, 3, 6–8, 10–12	$2.50
23–28	$250	*Mutant X*	
29, 30 JSA	$295	Marvel (1998–2001)	
31 Hawkman Joins	$225	1	$5
32–36, 40	$195	2–10	$3
37 1st SA Mr. Terrific	$250	11–32	$2.50
38 JSA	$225	*New Mutants*	
39 GS	$250	Marvel (1983–1991)	
41–45, 49, 50	$140	1	$10
46 JSA 1st SA Sandman	$250	2–10	$6
47 JSA	$160	11–20	$5
48 GS	$175	21–58	$4
51–54, 57, 59, 60	$125	59–61 Fall Mutants	$5
55 1st SA Earth-2 Robin	$175	62–85	$3
56 1st SA Wonder Woman	$175	86 1st Cable (cameo)	$15
58 GS	$150	87 1st full Cable	$35

88 Cable	$15		*Robocop*	
89–99	$5		Dark Horse	
100 last issue 52pp	$7		all Mini-Series cover price	
New Teen Titans			*Robocop*	
DC (1980–1984)			Marvel (1990–1992)	
1	$20		1 movie adaptation	$4
2 1st Deathstroke	$12		2–23	$2
3–10	$8		*Rocketeeer Adventure Mag, The*	
11–20	$5		Comico\Dark Horse	
21–40	$4		1 jul\88	$6
Nightwing			2 jul\89	$5
DC (1996–Present)			3 jan\95	$3
1	$15		*Rocketeer Special Edition, The*	
2	$10		Eclipse 1984	
3–10	$7		1	$10
11–25	$5		*Sandman*	
26 up	$2.50		DC (1974—75)	
Predator			1 1st Bronze Age App	$50
Dark Horse (1989–1990)			2–6	$20
1 movie adaptation 1st	$10		Volume 2 (Vertigo Imprint #47 up)	
2–4	$5		1989–1996	
Predator II			1	$25
Dark Horse (1991–1991)			2	$10
1 movie adaptation photo cover	$5		3–7, 9, 10	$8
2 photo cover	$4		8	$20
Punisher			11–20	$6
Marvel (1987–1995)			21–75	$5
Volume 2			*Showcase*	
1	$10		DC (1956–1978)	
2–10	$5		1 Fire Fighters	$5,000
11–20	$3		2 Kings Of The Wild	$1,250
21–100	$2.50		3 The Frogmen	$1,250
Volume 3 (April/2000–mar/2001)			4 1st, O SA Flash	$50,000
1	$6		5 Manhunters	$1,000
2–12	$3		6 1st, O Challengers of the	
Volume 4 (Aug/01–Present)			Unknown	$5,800
1	$5		7 Challengers of the Unknown	
2 up	$3			$2,500
Rising Stars			8 2nd Flash 1st Capt. Cold	$16,000
Image (1999–Present)			9 Lois Lane (before her own comic)	
0	$3			$10,000
1\2	$3		10 Lois Lane	$4,000
1	$5		11, 12 Challengers of the Unknown	
2–10	$3			$2,000
11 up	$2.50		13, 14 3rd, 4th Flash	$7,500
			15 1st Space Ranger	$2,500

16 Space Ranger	$1,250		80 1st Phantom Stranger	$125
17 1st Adam Strange	$4,200		81 Windy and Willy	$40
18, 19 Adam Strange	$1,950		82 1st Night Master	$100
20 1st Rip Hunter	$1,500		83 Night Master last 12¢ issue	$75
21 Rip Hunter	$650		84 Night Master	$65
22 1st, O SA Green Lantern	$7,500		85–87 Fire Hair, 88–90 Jason Quest,	
23, 24 Green Lantern	$3,000		91–93 Manhunter	$35
25, 26 Rip Hunter	$500		94 1st, O new Doom Patrol	$35
27 1st Sea Devils	$1,250		95, 96 Doom Patrol	$20
28, 29 Sea Devils	$625		97–99 Power Girl, 101–103	
30 O – SA Aquaman	$1,000		Hawkman, Adam Strange	$15
31–34 Aquaman	$650		100 52pp, 104 52pp last issue	$20

Star Trek

34 1st, O SA Atom	$2,100		**Star Trek**	
35 Atom last 10¢ issue	$1,200		Gold Key (1967–1979)	
36 Atom	$750		1	$700
37 1st Metal Men	$1,000		2	$300
38 Metal Men	$600		3–9	$200
39, 40 Metal Men	$500		10–30	$100
41, 42 O Tommy Tomorrow	$250		31–61	$50
43 Dr. No	$600		Marvel (1980–1982)	
44, 46, 47 Tommy Tomorrow	$175		1	$10
45 Sgt. Rock O retold	$395		2–5	$8
48, 49, 52 Cave Carson	$125		6–16	$6
50, 51 I Spy	$100		17, 18 low distribution	$15
53, 54 G.I. Joe	$150		DC (1984–1988)	
55 Dr. Fate and Hourman O both			1	$10
GA Green Lantern	$450		2–5	$8
56 Dr. Fate and Hourman	$250		6–20	$6
57 Enemy Ace	$275		21 up	$4
59 Teen Titans	$150		Volume 2 (1989–1996)	
60 1st SA Spectre	$425		1	$8
61, 64 Spectre	$200		2–5	$5
62 1st, O Inferior Five	$125		6–20	$4
63, 65 Inferior Five	$75		21 up	$3
66, 67 B'wana Beast	$50		**Star Wars**	
68 1st Maniaks	$75		Marvel (1977–1986)	
69, 71 Maniaks	$50		1	$50
70 Binky, 72 Top Gun	$50		1 (35¢ cover only 1500 copies)	$500
72 Top Gun	$40		2 4	$25
73 1st, O Creeper	$225		5–10	$20
74 1st Anthro	$100		11–20	$15
75 1st, O Hawk & Dove	$195		21–50	$12
76 1st Bat Lash	$95		51–90	$10
77 1st Angel and Ape	$75		91,93–99	$12
78 1st Jonny Double	$40		92,100 52pp	$20
79 1st Dolphin, O Aqualad	$95		101–106	$15

107 low distribution	$50
Annuals	
1 1979	$10
2 1982	$8
Dark Horse (1998–Present)	
1	$5
2–10	$4
11 up	$3
(All Dark Horse Star Wars mini series are cover price)	
Sub-Mariner Volume 2	
Marvel (1968–1974)	
1 O Sub-Mariner	$300
2	$125
3–10	$75
11–15 last 12¢ issue	$50
16–20	$30
21–33, 36–42	$18
34 Hulk, Silver Surfer	$50
35 versus Avengers	$40
43 52pp	$25
44, 45 Human Torch	$12
46–58, 60, 61, 63	$8
59 Thor	$15
62, 64–71	$6
72 last issue	$10
Special 1 1971	$15
Special 2 1972	$15
Superman	
DC (1939–1986)	
1	$250,000
2	$20,000
3	$10,000
4	$7,500
5	$6,000
30 1st Mr. Mxyztplk	$3,000
53 O Superman retold	$3,500
100	$2,500
101–110	$450
111–120	$400
121–130	$375
131–140	$325
141–145, 148	$225
146 Superman life story	$275
147 7th Legion App	$275
149 8th Legion App last 10¢ issue	

	$250
150–162	$175
163–182	$140
183, 187, 193, 197 GS	$150
184–186, 188–192, 198,	$125
199 Superman/Flash race	$350
200	$150
201, 203–206, 208–211, 213–216 last 12¢ issue	$75
218–220, 223–226, 228–231	$60
202, 207, 212, 217, 222 GS	$95
223–226, 228–231, 233–238	$40
227, 232, 239 GS	$75
240–248, 250, 251, 253, 245 100pp, all but 240 are 52pp	$45
249, 254 Nadams	$60
252 100pp reprints 5 GA comics	$75
255–271, 273–277, 279–283, 285	$25
272, 278, 284 100pg Giants	$45
286–299	$15
300	$25
301–350	$8
351–399	$5
400	$8
401–422	$4
423 last issue	$10
Annuals	
1 1960	$1,750
2 1960–61	$750
3 1961	$450
4 1961–62	$375
5, 6 1962, 1962–63	$300
7, 8 1963, 1963–64	$250
9 1964 80pg giant #1	$500
9–12 1983–86	$5
Volume 2 (1987–Present)	
1 Byrne Art	$10
2	$7
3–10	$5
11–15, 17–20, 21–49	$4
16 1st new Supergirl	$7
21 1st Matrix (new Supergirl)	$7
50	$5
51–99	$3

100	$4	95 GS	$75
101–122, 124 up	$2.50	101–103, 105–112, 114–120	
123 new costume	$5	last 12¢ issue	$30

Superman's Girl Friend Lois Lane
DC 1958–1974

1	$5,000	104, 113	$50
2	$1,500	121, 123–130,132	$20
3–5	$700	122, 131, 140	$40
6–10	$400	133 re-intro Newsboy Legion	$60
11–20	$250	134 1st Darkseid (cameo)	$100
21–29 last 10¢ issue	$175	135 2nd Darksied (cameo)	$50
30–50	$95	136–139	$30
51–67, 69	$75	141–150 52pp	$35
68 GS	$95	151–162	$15
70 1st SA Catwoman	$250	163 last issue	$20
71 Catwoman	$125		

72–76, 78–85, 87–92 last 12¢ issue	
	$50
77, 86 GS	$65
93 N. Adam's cover	$40
94,96–99,101–103, 106–111	$30
95 GS	$55
100	$40
104, 113 GS	$50
105 1st Rose and the Thorn	$65
112, 14–123 52pp	$25
124–136	$18
137 last issue	$25
Annuals	
1 1962	$325
2 1963	$200

Tales of Suspense
Marvel (1959–1968)

39 1st, O Iron Man	$7,000
40 2nd App	$2,500
41	$1,250
42–44	$725
45 1st Happy and Pepper,	
46 1st Crimson Dynamo	$450
47	$375
48 new Armor	$525
49 X-Men	$400
50 1st Mandarin	$300
51 1st Scarecrow	$225
52 1st Black Widow	$250
53 O The Watcher	$250
54–56	$135
57 1st, O Hawkeye	$300
58 1st Capt. America in this title	
	$395
59 1st 2 in one Iron Man &	
Capt. America Stories	$425
60 Hawkeye	$200
61, 62, 64, 67–70	$110
63 O Capt. America	$300
65 1st SA App, 66 O Red Skull	$200
71–98	$95
99 last issue becomes Capt. America	
	$110

Superman's Pal Jimmy Olsen
DC (1954–1974)

1	$7,500
2	$2,500
3 last pre-code issue	$1,250
4	$900
5	$750
6–10	$500
11–20	$350
21–31 (31 1st Elastic Lad,	
Jimmy Olsen)	$225
32–56 last 10¢ issue	$125
57–75	$75
76–94, 96–99	$50
100	$60

Tales to Astonish
Marvel (1959–1968)

27 1st Ant-Man last 10¢ issue	$6,000
28–34	$250
35 2nd Ant-Man	$2,500

36 Ant-Man	$1,000	21–26, 28–30	$50
37–40	$550	31–45, 47–50	$35
41–43, 49 becomes Giant Man	$425	46 O retold	$40
44 1st The Wasp	$525	51–57, 59–63, 65, 66	$30
45–48	$295	58 92pp	$40
50 1st Human Top	$195	64 100pp	$40
51, 53–56, 58	$175	67, 69, 71, 76–78 Barbara Leigh	
52 1st Black Knight	$210	photo covers	$40
57 Spider-Man	$250	68, 70, 72–75, 79–99	$25
59 Hulk	$295	100 96pp O retold	$75
60 1st 2 in one Giant Man and Hulk		101–110 low distribution	$50
Stories	$325	111, 112 both over size books	$65
61–69	$125	113 very low distribution	$300
70 Sub-Mariner and Hulk Begin		Annual #1 1972 Nadams	$300
	$165	Special #1 1977 softcover	$200
71–92	$95	#1 1977 hardcover	$500
93 Hulk VS Silver Surfer	$125	*Wolverine*	
94–99	$75	Marvel mini-series (1982)	
100	$85	1–4 Miller	$50
101 last issue	$125	Series (1988–Present)	
102 becomes Incredible Hulk		1	$50
Tomb Raiders		2	$25
Image/Top Cow (1999–Present)		3	$20
1	$5	4–9	$15
2	$3.50	10 1st Sabretooth battle	$25
3–10	$3	11–20	$10
11 up	$2.75	21–50	$8
Transformers, The		51–99	$5
Marvel (1984–1991)		100 ($3.95 cover)	$7.50
1	$15	($2.95 cover)	$5
2	$12	101–125	$3
3	$10	126 up	$2.50
4–10	$8	*Wonder Woman*	
11–70	$6	DC (1942–1986)	
71–79	$10	1 O retold	$32,000
80	$15	2 1st, O Mars	$5,000
Vampirella (mag)		3	$2,500
Warren Publishing (1969–1983)		6 1st Cheetah	$1,750
#113 Harris Pub.		45 O Wonder Woman retold	$1,000
1 1st	$650	70–79	$325
2	$225	80 O Invisible Plane	$350
3 low distribution	$500	81–97, 99	$250
4–9	$150	98 New O Wonder Woman	$300
10 no Vampirella	$50	100	$350
11–18, 20	$75	101–104, 106, 108–110	$225
19 1973 annual	$100		

105 O Wonder Woman (scarce)	$750		

105 O Wonder Woman (scarce) $750
107 1st Wonder Girl $275
111–126 last 10¢ issue $195
127–150 $110
151–158, 160–170 $75
159 O Wonder Woman retold $100
171–176, 179 $50
177 Wonder Woman VS Supergirl $95
178 1st new Wonder Woman $75
180 Death Steve Trever $60
181–195 $35
196 O Wonder Woman retold 52pp $50
197–200 52pp $45
201–210 $25
211, 214 100pp $50
212, 213, 215, 216, 218–220 $18
217 68pp $28
221–250 $12
251–270 $8
271–299 $6
300 $8
301–328 $4
329 last issue $10
Annuals
1 1988 $5
2 1989 $4
3–8 $3
Volume 2 (1987–Present)
1 New O $10
2 $7
3–10 $6
11–20 $5
21–50 $4
51–99 $3
100 $4
101 up $2.50

World's Best Comics
DC (1941)
1 Batman, Superman, Crimson Avenger and Johnny Thunder (100pp cardbord15¢ cover) $25,000

World's Finest Comics (continued from World's Best)
DC (1941–1986)
2 Superman and Batman $7,200
3 Sandman, Johnny Thunder 1st, O Scarecrow $4,200
4 $3,500
5 $3,200
6–10 $2,500
11–17 last cardboard cover $2,000
21–40 $1,200
41–64, 66–70 last 15¢ issue $725
65 O Superman $975
71 scarce 1st Superman/Batman team up 10¢ $1,200
72, 73 scarce $900
74 last pre–code, 75 1st code issue $750
76–83 $500
84–93, 94–99 $325
94 O Superman/Batman retold $750
100 $600
101–110 $225
111–121 last 10¢ issue $175
122–130 $125
131–150 $75
151–155, 157–160 $50
156 1st Bizarro Batman $95
161, 170 80pp $75
162–169, 171, 172, 174–178, 180–185 last 12¢ issue $35
173 1st SA Two-Face (Batman) $75
179 80pp $50
186, 187, 189–196, 201–203 $25
188, 197 64pp $35
98 $60
99 3rd Superman/Flash race $75
200 $30
204, 205, 207–212 52pp (208 48pp) $25
213–222, 229,231–243, 247, 248 $18
223–228 100pp $40
230 68pp $25
244–246, 249–252 84pp $22
253–265 $10

266–270, 272–282 52pp $12
271 O Superman/Batman Team 52pp
   $15
283–322 $6
323 last issue $9

X-Men (*Uncanny X-Men* 114 up)
Marvel (1963–Present)
1 1st X-Men $14,000
2 1st The Vanisher $3,500
3 1st Blob $1,300
4 1st Quick Silver and Scarlet Witch,
   1st Toad $1,400
5 Magneto and Evil Mutants $750
6, 8, 9 $595
7 Magneto $625
10 1st SA Ka-Zar and Zabu $625
11, 13–15 $495
12 1st Juggernaut $750
16–20 $325
21–27, 29, 30 $250
28 1st Banshee $325
31–34, 36–40 $175
35 Spider-Man $250
41–51, 53–55, 66 $150
52    $110
56, 57, 59, 60 Nadams $150
61–63, 65 Nadams $135
58 1st Havock Nadams $195
64 1st Sunfire $150
67–70 52pp reprints $95
71–93 reprints $75
94 New X-Men $1,200
95 Death of Thunderbird $325
96–99 $175
100, 101 O Storm $195
102–107, 109, 110 $125
108 Byrne art $175
111–119 $110
120 1st Alpha Flight $140
121 1st full Alpha Flight $160
122–128 $75
129 1st Kitty Pride $95
130 1st Dazzler $95
131–136, 138–140 $65

137 Double size death of Phoenix
   $75
141–143 last Byrne $60
144–157, 159, 160 $20
158 Rogue $30
161–170 $15
171 Rogue Joins the X-Men $18
172–174, 176–185, 187–192,
   194–199 $10
175, 186, 193, 186, 200 Double size
   $15
201 Cable $25
202–204, 206–209, 214–221,
   223–243, 247, 249, 250 $8
205 Wolverine story Barry Smith
   $18
210–213 $25
222 Wolverine Vs Sabretooth $30
244 1st Jubilee $40
248 1st Jim Lee X-Men $25
249–265 $8
266 1st Full Gambit $50
267 Gambit Jim Lee $20
268    $20
269–281 $7
282, 283 1st Bishop $15
284–299 $5
300    $7
301–303, 305–324, 326–350 $4
304, 324 $7
351–375 $3
376 up $2.50
Annuals/Specials
1 1970 $150
2 1971 $100
3 1979 $50
4, 5 1980–81 $18
6–8 1982–84 $10
11–13 $6
14 1990 1st Gambit $40
15 up $4
GS X-Men #1 1975 $1,500

Chapter 13:
Related Merchandise

In addition to movies, comic books also have a tremendous influence on other merchandise and vice-versa. This merchandise can be divided into both collectibles and usable items. Collectibles are items that have a buying public who want to buy and save specific items in top condition. These are expected to appreciate. Usable items are associated with comic book characters, and may be sold because of this. An example of this is a T-shirt with a picture of the Incredible Hulk on it.

A top ten list of related collectibles might contain the following:
1. Action Figures
2. Cards
3. Original artwork
4. Pez dispensers
5. Comic related statues
6. Lunch pails
7. Drinking glasses
8. Fasts food and cereal premiums
9. Books and novels
10. Other related toys and licensed products (with superhero image on them)

Usage items include such things as DVDs, Video Games, T-shirts, pillowcases, etc. The Spider-Man video game, for example, was the top seller for several months running on the Nintendo Game Cube and Sony Playstation 2. The strong popularity of these items is a reflection of a character's popularity and acceptance in society. This number ultimately reflects the attributes of a blue chip comic book.

We are beginning to collect prices for some of these items. These will appear in future issues of the book. Some of the most interesting comic-related collectibles are cards. These have demonstrated a massive popularity over the past few decades in a number of genres, including sports, television, movies and cartoons.

Manga and Anime Styles

Osamu Tezuka is recognized by many to be the Godfather of both of these styles of Japanese animation. Manga and Anime won fans in North America, Europe and the rest of the world with such television shows as *Astro Boy*, *Kimba-the White Lion* and *Prince Planet* in the 1960s. Since that time, more and more characters have become popular in North America based on Japanese art and animation including *Akira* by Katsuhiro Otomo and *Galaxy Express 999* by Rintaro. Other popular masterpieces include *The Blade of Kamui*, *Dragon Ball Z*, *Sailor Moon*, and *Pokemon*. New and popular characters and shows are being introduced to countries all over the world all the time.

Pokemon
Viz Comics
Comic book adaptation of the popular collecting cards.

Shogun Warriors 1
Marvel Comics
Shogun Warriors series – a gem from the 1970s that should appreciate significantly.

Manga/Anime 3 *Dragon Ball Z*
Viz Comics
Comic book adaptation of the popular collecting cards.

This art form has transcended the generation gap winning fans in all age groups and in both sexes. Fans enjoy the motion pictures and cartoon shows. Manga is known as the Japanese comic. Hobbyists also collect cards, games, and toys based on Manga characters. Anime is based on specific techniques for drawing male and female eyes, noses, mouths, facial expressions and the shape of a character's head in animation.

Manga plays a strong role in Japanese culture. These comic books are written for everyone in many different styles. They generally portray society and technology working together. There is almost always a philosophical or spiritual theme.

Collector cards, based on characters such as Yu Gi Oh!, Digimon and Pokemon have an enormous following and have become major collector's items. Here is a brief description on Yu Gi Oh! and Digimon and some collector card samples.

Yu Gi Oh!

The beginning of the story of Yu Gi Oh was a dark pharaoh that locked up things that are called millennium items. These were unlocked by a boy named Yu Gi. He also unlocked something called dueling and it is used with very powerful cards. When Yu Gi unlocked the millennium items, he obtained a millennium puzzle and in that puzzle he obtained another soul that is very good at dueling.

People collect the dueling cards to become the greatest dueler in the world. The cards are valuable because each of them has their own personality, power, and effects that make them powerful. People collect cards with a power level and the goal is to get a card with at least a 2000 power level because those cards are usually very rare and contain a special attack.

Cards are bought at game stores. They can be purchased in booster packs, decks and starter decks (3 hollow cards and 47 plain cards). The characters on the hollow cards are stronger than those on the plain cards based on effect, attack and defense power. Everyone wants a card name Exodia. It is made up of 5 cards that are very rare.

Digimon

Every Digimon has a special power. The objective is to become a Digimon trainer. Digimon hatch from eggs and are originally from the Digital world. The essence of this story is that good Digimon protect their partners and fight the bad Digimon.

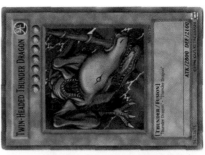

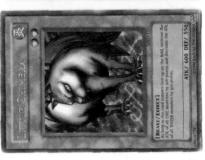

Left:
Digimon
Set
Nintendo
A collection
of Digimon
cards.

Right: *Yu*
Gi Oh! **set**
Kazuki
Takahashi
A collection
of cards.

Xena set
Topps
A collection of Xena cards.

Xena 1
Topps
Xena ready for action.

Ms. Marvel 1
Marvel
Captured ideas from the women's movement in the 1970s.

Ms. Mystic #1
PC
A highly anticipated book that unfortunately suffered from lots of publication delays.

Supergirl #1
DC Comics
The Supergirl character is still waiting for a breakout event.

Spider-Woman V1 #1
Marvel Comics
1st appearance of Spider-Woman.

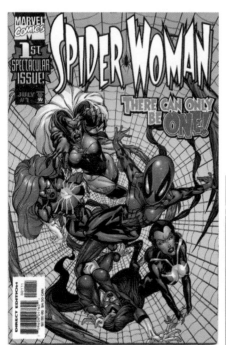

Spider-Woman V2 #2
Marvel Comics
Volume 2 series starring
Spider-Man.

Stan Lee's *Wonder Woman*
DC Comics
Wonder Woman looks good no
matter who's writing the story.

Updated version of *Wonder Woman*
DC Comics
What did we say about Wonder
Woman already?

Vampirella
Harris Comics
Vampirella has a strong fan
following. Bloody good fun.

Wild Thing 1
Marvel Comics
Wolverine's daughter – scary.

Spider-Girl
Marvel Comics
The daughter of Spider-Man.

Black Cat 1
Marvel Comics
From the pages of Spider-Man
into her own series.

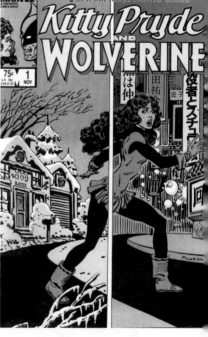

Kitty Pryde 1
Marvel Comics
1st appearance was in *X-Men*
139.

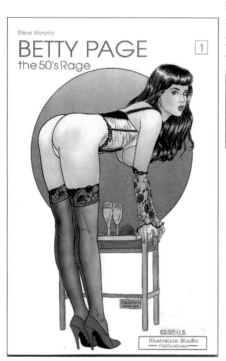

Betty Page
Illustration Studios
From the 1950s into the
modern age – a bit of
naughtiness.